CONSULTATIVE SELLING TECHNIQUES FOR FINANCIAL PROFESSIONALS

Karl F. Gretz
Steven R. Drozdeck

NEW YORK INSTITUTE OF FINANCE

Library of Congress Cataloging-in-Publication Data

Gretz, Karl F.
    Consultative selling techniques for financial professionals/Karl
F. Gretz, Steven R. Drozdeck.
      p. cm.
   ISBN 0-13-083445-9
   1. Financial services industry. 2. Brokers. 3. Insurance—
Agents. 4.Selling—Banks and banking. 5. Selling. I. Drozdeck,
Steven R. II. Title.
HG173.G74   1990
332.1′068′8—dc20   89-29853
                                       CIP

This publication is designed to provide accurate and authoritative information in regard to the subject matter covered. It is sold with the understanding that the publisher is not engaged in rendering legal, accounting, or other professional service. If legal advice or other expert assistance is required, the services of a competent professional person should be sought.

From a Declaration of Principles Jointly Adopted by
a Committee of the American Bar Association and a
Committee of Publishers and Associations

© 1990 by Karl F. Gretz and Steven R. Drozdeck
Published by NYIF Corp.
A Division of Simon & Schuster, Inc.
2 Broadway, New York, NY 10004-2207

Printed in the United States of America
10 9 8 7 6 5 4 3 2 1

New York Institute of Finance
(NYIF Corp.)

This book is sincerely dedicated to those people without whose help and support it could not have come about: first, the Gretz and Drozdeck families, who put up with us while it was being written and encouraged us in a thousand and one ways; and second, Joseph A. Ross, Ph.D., who is more responsible than anyone else for raising the level of professionalism in brokerage training.

Contents

Preface

If you are involved in retail sales in securities, insurance, or banking, this book is written for you. Both authors were successful account executives at Merrill Lynch before they became sales trainers for the firm. The authors also have experience in selling retail products from all three financial areas. In addition, they have been successful and effective consultants to Fortune 500 companies in sales and communications. Between them, they have trained over 15,000 sales and management personnel in the psychology and art of selling for major securities, insurance, and banking corporations.

This book is the result of an effort to bring together selling and communication skills developed over years of experience as brokers, trainers, and consultants, as well as to draw on the insights and suggestions of fellow professionals. We acknowledge and sincerely thank those individuals who have been of tremendous help to us in the development and publication of the book. Joseph A. Ross, Ph.D., supported the idea of the book from the beginning and helped to edit and clarify it. He was also instrumental in our finding a publisher. Betsy Brown, our editor, went above and beyond the call of duty many times to help us. And Sandy Buchanan, Robert Clark, Dolores Gibson, Art Mortel, Ernesto C. Pallesco, Michael J. Ryan, Todd Taylor, and James Wilkerson reviewed all or parts of the manuscript and gave us excellent suggestions and support.

Introduction

Consultative Selling Techniques for Financial Professionals is unlike other sales books because of its unique perspective. It does not inundate you with techniques designed to manipulate the client into a quick sale. Such techniques don't really work. They may sound magnificent; but, at best, they are a temporary crutch that is useful mainly as a motivational tool.

This book is different. It offers you an opportunity to learn about how people think and react on both an unconscious and a conscious level. Once you realize that 85 to 90 percent of all real communication and sales take place below the conscious level of awareness, you can learn approaches that will ensure that you are perceived positively by your prospects and clients.

Have you ever purchased something from a friend? Have you ever gone to a particular store because you like the salesperson? Ask a few of your friends and associates these questions and you'll realize the extent to which people prefer to buy from their friends.

People genuinely like to do business with people they like. They will actually go out of their way to accommodate a friend. "Let's buy it from Joe down the street," someone might say, even though doing so may involve paying a small premium. "After all, Joe is a friend. He'd help us."

Much has been written about the characteristics of star performers in sales. The attributes are quite consistent regardless of the particular industry. Robert Shook wrote an interesting book entitled *Ten Greatest Salespersons—What They Say About Selling.* Among the many characteristics he presented, we find that two merit special attention:

1. Successful salespeople have an almost intuitive knowledge of their clients' psychological needs.
2. Clients like successful salespeople as friends.

These two characteristics are the end result of the development of certain skills and attributes, which are the focus of this book.

We present them using the "consultative sales" approach, which has become widely recognized as the most effective and efficient method of establishing and maintaining long-term client relationships. *Long-term* is a key word in this book, for we are writing with the assumption that *you want additional business,* that *you want repeat business,* that *you want referrals,* and that *you and your company want satisfied customers.* Finally, we are assuming that you want to emulate the top performers. If our assumptions are correct, then read on.

It was stated earlier that understanding the psychological needs of clients and being liked by clients are the two crucial characteristics of successful salespeople. The first trait—understanding clients' psychological needs—is both within your control and something you can learn. The second—being liked by your clients—may *seem* to be outside your control, but really isn't. You can learn how to influence an individual subconsciously so that it is virtually assured he or she will like you. We will discuss more about each of these skills later.

This book presents a nonstandard approach to selling: *You will learn the "how tos" behind all the "you shoulds" presented in other books and courses.* Other books and courses say "you should gain the client's confidence," "you should develop rapport," "you ought to do this and/or that." We will provide you with the skills necessary to build that all-important relationship with your clients!

The book is divided into eight major sections. Section One presents the basic ideas of the book, including personal skills and attributes that are common to highly successful financial professionals. Section Two deals with essential communication skills and methods you can use to immediately enhance your effectiveness. It also highlights the key terms that are used throughout the work.

The basics of psychological profiling are presented in the third section. Here you'll learn about general personality traits and how they apply to your clients. This information will enable you to develop your presentations more precisely. You'll also learn how to effectively manage various types of clients. This information will prove useful outside of business, for the techniques we offer are applicable to virtually any relationship you may have. *You'll find that the skills presented in this book have universal application.*

How to achieve rapport with anyone in five minutes—the same depth of rapport it normally takes three to five hours to attain using hit-or-miss methods—is the subject of Section Four. The premise of this section is: People like those who are most like themselves—literally and figuratively. We provide a step-by-step method of establishing, maintaining, and enhancing rapport. You will learn state-of-the-art physical and psychological techniques.

"The Art of Telephone Prospecting" is the subject of Section Five. The title is a slight misnomer because the skills are applicable to anyone who uses the telephone in the normal course of business, but those who use the telephone to find new business prospects will derive tremendous benefit from this section.

Effective selling is dependent on fully understanding the client's needs and wants. How to easily, casually, and efficiently obtain this extremely valuable information (and presell your next sale in the process) is the purpose of Section Six—"Profiling."

The seventh section describes a very effective sales methodology. Incorporating the information from previous sections, we present a systematic approach to sales that makes a "no" decision by the client highly unlikely. This extremely persuasive sequence is accompanied by rationales so that you will be able to make adaptations where necessary.

The final section tells you how to handle stress. Your

ability to maintain motivation, enthusiasm, effectiveness, and success very much depends on how you handle the day-to-day stresses of your job. In fact, "burnout" is one of the most common causes of failure and, once experienced, is difficult to overcome. However, it is relatively simple to avoid *if* you follow the simple steps for managing stress provided in Section Eight.

The six appendices cover such topics as: responses to typical stalls and objections; exercises for mastery of topics presented in key chapters; profiling questions; statements to generate prospect interest; sources of prospect lists; and forms that will enable you to evaluate your performance.

For further information on available courses, tapes, and workbooks, contact the authors at:

Gretz Associates
Corporate Consulting
4431 Remo Crescent Drive
P.O. Box 1457
Bensalem PA 19020
(215) 639–1922

GETTING STARTED

By beginning a career as a representative of a bank, brokerage firm, a mutual fund, an insurance company, or a financial planning firm, you have taken one of the most exciting steps of your life. In this career, you will be able to help hundreds of people obtain financial security for themselves, their companies, and their heirs and dependents. There is no other career in the world in which you can make as much money helping so many people in so short a time.

In 1933, Congress enacted the Glass-Steagall Act, which prohibited commercial banks from owning brokerage firms. In the mid-1980s, banks challenged this Act by offering several financial services traditionally reserved to brokerage firms. As a result of the continuing erosion of regulations separating the functions of banks, brokerage houses, and insurance firms, you face a tremendous increase in the amount of competition for each dollar of your client's assets. Today, regardless of the type of firm for which you work, you can offer a wide variety of products and services that were previously controlled by your competition. For example:

- Insurance companies now sell mutual funds.
- Banks sell stocks, bonds, insurance, and mutual funds in addition to their traditional fare.
- Brokerage houses sell virtually everything, from stocks and bonds to bank certificates of deposit, mutual funds, insurance, and savings accounts.

We will provide examples utilizing a variety of financial products and services from the banking, insurance, and brokerage industries. Most readers will be able to adapt our examples to their particular situation, while those working in the brokerage industry should find virtually all of the examples applicable to them.

For your reading ease, we have opted to refer to the position of sales representative as "financial consultant" (FC). We have done this because no matter which arm of the financial services industry you represent, your clients consult with you on some aspect of their finances.

We have included an important aid to your getting as much as possible out of this book. Throughout the text you will see the most important aspects of consultative selling highlighted in boxes. These boxes contain catchphrases that summarize, in quick and easy-to-remember words, the focus of the preceding text. Whenever you are faced with confusion or doubt, refer to these boxes and you'll soon find you can easily remember each integral part of the system.

CHAPTER 1

The Character of Success

Think of some of the great men and women of history: Thomas Jefferson, George Washington, Thomas Edison, George Washington Carver, Susan B. Anthony, Theodore Roosevelt, Eleanor Roosevelt, Benjamin Franklin, Simon Bolivar, and Madame Curie. What was it that made them great? Was it intelligence coupled with opportunity? Hardly. While all were intelligent, many had little opportunity when they began. The single common denominator of their greatness was character. They accomplished what they did because of their character.

Developing Character

What is "character"? Most of us have achieved what we have today through a series of accidents. That may sound pretty strong, but think about it. An accident of birth placed us in the homes where we were nurtured. And our characters were formed as a result of meeting and being influenced by certain people. We developed our character through a process of osmosis, absorbing bits of it from our associates. Amazing, isn't it? Yet almost all the people we have asked (so far, over 5,000) have admitted that they have given almost no thought to the planning or the development of their character.

Young children have little conscious control over their character development. They accept what they see and hear from parents, relatives, teachers, and friends without question. They use little or no evaluation to determine the validity of an idea or an action. They seldom stop to consciously judge whether a new idea will intermesh with everything else they have learned. Despite this, two of the great things about human beings are our ability to consciously determine which character traits we wish to have and our subsequent systematic work to attain them. That is how the men and women mentioned above achieved greatness.

Lack of Character

One of the chief causes of failure in the financial services industry is lack of character. Most of the people who fail simply give up and quit because a career in this field requires more work than they had planned on. Many others fail because they lack the self-discipline to organize their time and goals and to stick with the tasks required for success. Additionally, a few fail because they give a higher priority to immediate profits than to their clients' welfare. In a word, there are many roads to both failure and success, but all roads to success require work and self-discipline.

Setting Character Goals

In Chapter 3, we'll discuss your need to set goals and determine what resources you need to attain those goals. Since the single most important resource for real success is character, it is important to set character development goals as well as material goals. Then you will not only achieve material success, but will also be proud of the person who accomplished that success.

Benjamin Franklin is generally considered to be one of the greatest men who ever lived. He helped frame the Declaration of Independence and the Constitution, was our first ambassador to both England and France, established the first fire department and post office, discovered electricity, and invented bifocals and the Franklin stove. Not bad when you consider that at age twenty he was a printer's apprentice with few prospects.

What happened to him? How did someone with so little going for him achieve such greatness? When he was a young man, Franklin realized that if he was to amount to anything, he would have to work to develop his character.

To begin with, he determined thirteen character traits that he thought were critical to greatness. These included:

- *Silence:* Speak not but what may benefit others or yourself. Avoid trifling conversation.
- *Order:* Let all your things have their places. Let each part of your business have its time.
- *Resolution:* Resolve to perform what you ought. Perform without fail what you resolve.
- *Industry:* Lose no time. Be always employed in something useful. Cut off all unnecessary actions.
- *Sincerity:* Use no harmful deceit. Think innocently and justly; and if you speak, speak accordingly.
- *Justice:* Wrong none by doing injuries or omitting the obligations that are your duty.

You may choose different character traits—perhaps integrity, promptness, temperance—that you feel are appropriate for you.

Next, Franklin wrote down the traits and defined what each one meant to him. Your definitions of character traits need to include observable behavior. If you achieve a given trait, would someone else be able to tell so from observing your behavior?

Then Franklin spent a week on each trait. For an entire week, he focused on living his definition of that particular trait. At the end of each day, he would review his progress and rate himself: Had he improved, remained the same, or fallen back? At the end of the week, he would review his progress for the week and then focus on the next trait.

He spent a week on each character trait for thirteen weeks, then began again. He did this for over sixty years. It's not hard to see how he made a *habit* of developing a winning character.

BUILDING CHARACTER REQUIRES GOOD HABITS!

Perseverance

President Calvin Coolidge made the point excellently when he proclaimed that, to succeed, you have to stick to it and never give up. He said:

> Press on. Nothing in the world can take the place of persistence. Talent will not: Nothing is more common than unsuccessful men with talent. Genius will not: Unrewarded genius is almost a proverb. Education alone will not: The world is full of educated derelicts. Persistence and determination alone are omnipotent.

Perseverance is also a character trait. But unless you have a strong character, the time may come when you find it impossible to resist the "opportunity" to cut corners in order to make a quick profit. For example, some people suggest that it is all right to lie to secretaries if that will enable you to get past them to prospect their boss. There are two good reasons for ignoring such spurious advice:

1. There is no way that you can lie fifty times a day and not have it affect your relationship with your family and with yourself.
2. When a client realizes that you have lied once, he will never trust you again.

Summary

Consider the great and successful individuals in your life, the people you admire and would like to emulate. Explore the character traits that you think have made them successful. Choose the traits you want to have yourself and make a habit of living them. In the end, you'll make more money and be a lot happier. Remember that everything you do or say, or fail to do or say, communicates something about you. What do you want communicated?

Exhibit 1-1 presents a form that will help you to crystalize your thinking as you explore the traits you wish to develop or enhance in yourself. Using it, first list the trait and then the benefits that you hope to obtain by developing or strengthening that trait in yourself.

This form will get you started on six traits. Eventually,

EXHIBIT 1-1
The Character of My Success.

Character Trait	*Benefits*
1. _____	_____
2. _____	_____
3. _____	_____
4. _____	_____
5. _____	_____
6. _____	_____

you may wish to add more. To paraphrase Og Mandino, the author of *The Greatest Salesman in the World:*

> As in life itself, I realize that the amount of success I am able to achieve through my character will be in direct proportion to the effort I expend in developing it.

In the next three chapters, we will explore effective techniques for getting started, setting goals, and managing your time. Section Two goes on to explore ways to make certain that what you communicate is what you *want* to communicate.

CHAPTER 2

Getting Down to Business

Almost anyone who is sufficiently well motivated and willing to consistently follow a few simple rules can succeed as a financial consultant (FC). It is important to recognize this. Mere talent or intelligence is not enough. Hard, consistent work is the key to success in the financial services industry. As Coach Lavelle Edwards of Brigham Young University put it, "If you see a man on the top of a mountain, you can be pretty sure that he didn't fall there."

You must develop three important characteristics if you are to succeed:

1. You must be **efficient** (use your time wisely and do things right the first time—see Chapter 4).
2. You must be **effective** (set goals and do the right things—see Chapter 3.
3. You must **persevere!**

New Competition

Thirty years ago, the financial services industries (especially banking and brokerage) were heavily regulated and there was little competition. You could survive on inherited accounts and wait for new business to come to you. Those days are long gone. Today most FCs recognize the need to get out and actively seek business.

Deregulation isn't the only change to come to the industry. As John Naisbitt made clear in his bestseller *Megatrends,* the advent of "The Age of Information" has resulted in a significantly better-informed and more service-oriented public. Just five years ago, it was possible to find clients who were willing to invest significant quantities of money on the advice of a faceless voice on the phone. Today such clients are not only harder to find, but are more likely to litigate when they are disappointed by investment performance.

With deregulation, your competition consists of all other financial services companies (other brokerage houses, mutual fund companies, banks, insurance companies, and even credit unions). Each is competing for your client's investment business. What's worse, they are looking to tie up the client's real assets and credit as well. This means that today you must work much harder to provide professional service and to develop a relationship with each and every customer. If you don't, someone else will, and your clients will move their business.

You've probably heard that there are only two ways to make more money in this business: either obtain new clients or increase the amount of business you do with existing clients. The most successful FCs do both. Consistent prospecting as well as asking for referrals will increase your client base. At the same time, constantly offering additional services will increase the amount of your clients' assets that are under your management.

Many firms have done studies showing a direct correlation between financial consultants' commission revenue and the amount of client assets they directly manage (more assets equals more commission revenues). Similarly, studies have shown that increasing the number of products and services provided to a client raises an FC's chances of keeping that client. For example, in 1986, the Chicago Board Options Exchange did a study of 10,000 customers that produced the results shown in Exhibit 2-1. Consequently, it is important to gather as much of your clients' assets as possible under your management. Every

EXHIBIT 2-1

No. of Products/Services with Customer	Chance of Keeping Customer for One Year
1	33%
2	67%
3 or more	83%

dollar that remains with someone else provides that competitor with a "hook" that can be used to pull your customer away from you. Hence, it is no longer sufficient to specialize in stocks, or bonds, or some other specific product or service. You must understand at least the basics of a wide variety of the financial products and services available to meet your clients' needs.

In addition, you may frequently be called upon to convince your customer of the superiority of your product or service. As a professional, you will need to know the features, advantages, and benefits (FABs) of your competitors' products and services as well as your own.

Remember, this is *your* business. You decide how hard you will work, which products you will sell, whom you will seek out as clients, how much you will be paid, and, ultimately, how successful you will be.

Preparation

Several simple rules for managing your business have proven consistently successful to FCs across the board.

- It is very important to be highly organized. Otherwise the amount of information that will cross your desk in a period of just a few days will become overwhelming. (Organization will be discussed in subsequent sections.)
- Before coming to the office each morning, it is useful to have lists of: (a) qualified prospects (see Section Five, "The Art of Telephone Prospecting," and Appendix 2 for information on where to find prospecting lists), and (b) customers whose profiles show they have needs you can meet (see Section Six, "Profiling," and Appendix 5 for profiling questions).

- Come in early. Many executives are at their desks by 7:00 A.M., when there is no secretary screening their calls. They answer their own phones and are frequently more receptive at that hour.

- Studies show that "cold calling" is like a marathon. For every one hundred calls that you make, you should open at least one account (see Section Five, "The Art of Telephone Prospecting"). So pace yourself, and try for at least one hundred contacts each day. (*Note:* Because of the constant rejection in cold calling, many potentially successful FCs "burn out" and leave the business. See Section Eight, "Managing Stress in Today's Financial Marketplace," for ways to deal with on- and off-the-job pressure.)

- Successful FCs consistently work overtime at least two to three nights per week for the first two or three years in the business. You will probably want to consider what effect this will have on your personal life, especially if you have a family. In Section Eight, we suggest ways to ensure that your needs and those of your family are met during this period of extra work.

- Set concrete long-, intermediate-, and short-term goals and keep to them (see Chapter 3, "Effective Goal Setting"). It may also be useful to meet with your sales manager to determine what expectations he or she has for your production.

- Study every aspect of your new career, from the economy to your competition, for at least an hour a day during the first three years. Know your firm's products and services and how they compare with the competition's.

- Remember that you are a professional whose "reason for being" is to help your clients. If you do this, the commissions will take care of themselves.

- Avoid selling investments that require you to spend too much time staring at stock quotations instead of calling new prospects.

Organization

We cannot overemphasize the importance of keeping yourself and your work organized if you are to succeed. As obvious as this may appear, it is remarkable how many new FCs fail because they have difficulty organizing their work and controlling the flow of information with which they must deal.

Over the course of your career, hundreds of pages of information will cross your desk every day. You must develop a system for quickly determining which data are useful now, which should be saved, which should be disseminated to clients, and which should be discarded. Without such a system from the start, you may find yourself overwhelmed (see Chapter 4, "Time Management").

Keep a Clean Desk

A clean desk is critical to maintaining control of the information flow for which you are responsible. We once knew a broker whose desk was so covered with papers that it was impossible to see its surface. When a new manager finally forced him to clean it, he found paperwork going back ten years. Not surprisingly he had made more costly errors in sales than anyone else in the office.

Organize your materials to minimize the number of things on your desk. Some objects to keep on your desk are:

• Your stock quote machine
• Your phone
• The list of people (prospects and clients) that you are calling
• The script that you are using to call them
• Your phone log

Too many papers are a distraction that could cost you a lot of money.

Avoid eating at your desk! If you want a snack or lunch, get up, get it, and finish it before you sit down again. The unconscious mind labels areas as workplaces, eating places, et cetera. Even a cup of coffee at your desk can leave embarrassing rings on important papers. If you are to be at your most efficient, your mind must be programmed to work from the moment you sit down.

ORGANIZATION IMPROVES EFFICIENCY AND INCOME!

REMEMBER: To succeed, you must develop three important characteristics:

- You must be **efficient.**
- You must be **effective.**
- You must **persevere!**

Effective Goal Setting

William James, one of the founders of modern psychology, once said, "What the mind can conceive, it can achieve." Our conceptions can become our goals. However, before a goal can become a motivating, dynamic source of power, it must meet several criteria.

* *Always write your goals down.* In 1950, the Ivy League Colleges began a study of that year's graduating classes. In answer to the question whether they had established goals for their lives, 87 percent of the graduates said that they had not. Ten percent said they had established mental goals, but had not written them down, and only 3 percent said they had developed written goals for their lives.

  The schools followed the progress of their graduates for twenty-five years. In 1975, they found the following: the 87 percent who had not established goals had performed in an average manner during the intervening twenty-five years. After attending the most expensive schools in the country, these people had achieved *mediocrity*. The 10 percent who had established mental goals but had not written them down had outperformed the

87 percent of their classmates without goals. The 3 percent who had developed written goals had outperformed the other 97 percent of their classmates combined!

- *Goals must be stated positively:* what you want to achieve, rather than what you want to avoid. For example: "I want to cold-call one hundred new contacts each day" (positive), instead of "I want to stop being so afraid of the telephone" (negative). (*Note:* For more on this, see Chapter 18, "Think and Speak Positively.")

- *Your goals must be within your control.* For example, wanting to gather X millions of dollars in assets in new accounts each year is possible. That is under your control. Wishing to grow six inches taller is not. Each goal you set should be challenging but realistic. Goals that are virtually impossible to achieve will only discourage you and sap your will to continue. At the other extreme, goals that are too easy are boring and quickly lose their ability to motivate.

  Select goals that you can achieve, but only by stretching yourself. If you find that you are achieving a goal too easily, make your next goal harder. If, on the other hand, you are becoming frustrated at the inherent difficulty of a goal, consider first if you are working efficiently toward achieving it (see Chapter 4, "Time Management"). If you are, move the goal a little closer.

- *Each goal must be testable in some objective manner.* For example, if your goal is to be able to afford a certain kind of new car or house, it is easy to test whether you have achieved it.

- *Be sure that you understand each goal.* For example, if your goal is to obtain a certain level of income, make sure you know how much production is required to attain that income. What kinds of order tickets must you write to achieve that production? How many and what kinds of clients must you have to write those tickets? How much prospecting must you do to obtain those clients? And so on.

- *Your goal should not cost more than it is worth.* Let's say that your goal is to achieve $1 million in income during your first year of production. You may be able to accomplish this, but it may cost you your family, your integrity, and/or your health. Would it be worth it? The number of unhappy, unhealthy, divorced million-dollar producers is too great to ignore.

Does this mean that you shouldn't develop great goals? Of course not. There are a great number of very happy, healthy million-dollar producers who have very satisfying family lives. To avoid having success cost more than it is worth, we suggest that you ask yourself a few simple questions about each goal you are considering.

- Be sure that it is *your* goal rather than something you think is expected of you by your parents, peers, or society. Naturally, you must fulfill the expectations of your company to remain employed. However, trying to live up to other people's expectations has caused more stress and more burnout than almost any other factor.
- What will change in your life if you obtain this goal? Will it be for the better? For the worse? Always remember that every goal has a price.
- How will you know when you have achieved your goal?
- When, where, and with whom do you wish to attain your goal?
- What will happen if you obtain your goal? What will happen if you don't? The second question is particularly important because how you feel about *not* attaining a goal is a large factor in how stressful the effort toward that goal becomes. It also determines how effective this goal will be in motivating you.
- Related to the previous question is: How do you know if your goal is really worth obtaining? Did someone else tell you? How does that person know?
- What is stopping you, or what might stop you, from obtaining your goal? What obstacles do you face?
- Finally, what resources will you require to overcome these obstacles and achieve your goal?

Long-Range, Intermediate, and Short-term Goals

Most of us think primarily in terms of long-range goals, forgetting the importance of the milestones we pass on the way to achieving those goals. For example, you may have a long-range goal of becoming a million-dollar producer. But right now that may look almost impossible simply because it is too big or too far away.

Have you ever heard the old joke about how to eat an elephant? The punch line is: "One bite at a time." Becoming a million-dollar producer is no different. However, even taken in bites, an elephant can be a bit daunting. But how about the elephant's leg? That's only one chunk of elephant. Given enough time, you could surely eat just the leg. That's how we establish intermediate- and short-term goals—we "chunk down."

Chunking down is the process of breaking a large goal into pieces that are small enough to handle. Large pieces become milestones, or intermediate goals, that tell us we have made significant progress toward our long-range goal. Small pieces become short-term goals that tell us we are making progress toward our intermediate goals. Each bite could be a daily goal.

It is important to break a goal down in a manner that will motivate you and show you that you can achieve your desired result. If your chunks are too small, you risk boredom or the feeling that you will never reach the end. If they are too large, you may become frustrated and discouraged.

In addition to specific chunks, you need to include in your plans whatever resources you require to achieve your goal. Resources must be included in your short-term and intermediate chunks as well. What skills and knowledge will you need to become a million-dollar producer? Make the obtaining of those skills and knowledge goals in themselves. Then break these goals down into manageable chunks.

Setting a Time Frame

The most effective way to determine if you are on track is to monitor your progress along the road to "success" (i.e., achieving your goal). We've already discussed the importance of placing milestones on the road. Now let's look at setting up a time frame for accomplishing each goal.

If you establish a goal without setting a specific time within which to accomplish it, you have given it the lowest priority. (We'll discuss priorities in more detail in Chapter 4, "Time

Management.'') After all, not setting a time requirement for something implies that you have ''all the time in the world'' to do it. How much effort do you currently put into accomplishing something that has no specific deadline? We all need a sense of urgency to motivate us and to help us to determine which tasks must be completed first.

The problem with long-range goals is that they are so far in the future that there seems to be no reason to put them first today. By breaking down a long-range goal into intermediate- and short-term goals, we increase not only our sense of urgency, but also our sense of accomplishment and movement toward the long-term goal. Therefore, whenever you set a goal, establish a time frame for accomplishing it. Long-term goals take usually five to ten years, intermediate goals one to five years, and short-term goals six months to one year. Keep in mind that any goal can be divided into shorter-term interim goals. Even a six-month goal can, and probably should, be broken down into monthly, weekly, and perhaps daily goals.

For example, let's take a look at what your interim goals might be if becoming a million-dollar producer is your long-range goal. Achieving this goal might represent being able to afford a certain lifestyle, or to support a favorite worthy cause, or to be free of worry about providing for your children's education. You might establish your priorities as follows:

- **Long-term Goal:** MILLION-DOLLAR PRODUCTION. **Time frame:** 5 years. **Requirements:**

    Assets: Figuring a production credit of 1 percent of total assets under management, you need to develop an asset base of at least $100 million.

    Accounts: If your *average* account has $100,000, you must obtain at least 1,000 accounts to gain the necessary assets to manage.

    Skills: To obtain and maintain 1,000 large accounts, you must have a thorough knowledge of your business, including your company's products and services (such as stocks and bonds, options, insurance, retirement and pension plans, financial planning); the competition; tax laws, and the state of the economy. You must also understand how to determine what products and services will solve a customer's financial problem and how to sell them to that customer.

- **Intermediate Goal:** year 4. $700,000 in production. Requires: at least 700 accounts of $100,000 or more so as to equal $70 million in assets under management.

- **Intermediate Goal:** year 3. $450,000 in production. Requires: at least 450 accounts of $100,000 or more ($45 million in assets under management). Necessary knowledge: a thorough understanding of all your company's products and services that might affect your clients and completion of a course in financial planning.

- **Intermediate Goal:** year 2. $250,000 in production. Requires: at least 250 accounts of $100,000 or more ($25 million in assets under management). Necessary knowledge: a strong familiarity with the basics of your company and the brokerage business; an insurance license; comprehension of what your competition offers; a solid understanding of the economy; and completion of the first half of a course in financial planning.

- **Intermediate Goal:** year 1. $100,000 in production. Requires: at least 100 accounts of $100,000 or more ($10 million in assets under management). Necessary knowledge: a good understanding of how your company works and where to go for information and assistance when your client has a financial requirement you do not know how to handle.

- **Short-term Goal:** 6 months. $35,000 in production. Requires: at least 35 accounts of $100,000 or more ($3.5 million in assets under management).

- **Short-term Goal:** 3 months. $12,000 in production. Requires: at least 12 accounts of $100,000 or more ($1.2 million in assets under management).

Be aware of "lag time." It takes an average of three weeks to three months from your first contact with a prospect to get that person to open an account. In addition, there may be a lag between gathering assets and actual production. However, once the assets are in, production follows.

The production numbers that we provided above are not completely accurate. They are based upon an average figure of 1 percent of assets under management. For new assets, however, the figure is closer to 2.5 percent of total asset dollars. Therefore, it is possible to achieve first-year production of $250,000 with $10 million under management. Just remember that, especially at first, all of your new accounts will not be $100,000 or larger. Thus you will want to obtain many more than 100 new accounts in your first year.

Be sure to break your goals down into monthly, weekly, and daily chunks. To reach that figure of $10 million in assets your first year, you will need to open between 200 and 300 new accounts, or an average of at least one a day. In the chapter on prospecting, we'll discuss just how to do this. Always ask yourself: Is what I'm doing *now* moving me toward one of my goals?

Daily Focus

Set daily goals for yourself and keep track of them (this is also discussed in the chapters on managing stress). For example, make a "tick sheet' each day to keep track of your cold calls and their effectiveness. Set a goal of a specific number of calls, or contacts, every day, then keep track of how many you actually make and what percentage become prospects. Exhibit 3-1 is an example of such a sheet. You may wish to design one that meets your specific goals and to make copies of it.

A personal tick sheet will tell you the progress that you are making toward each day's goal. It will also provide information regarding the effectiveness of the lists you are calling and the prospecting scripts you are using.

Remember that if you don't have a goal, any direction you go in will seem as good as another.

> ## GOALS GIVE DIRECTION TO YOUR DRIVE FOR SUCCESS!

EXHIBIT 3-1

Dials: ̶I̶H̶T̶ ̶I̶H̶T̶ ̶I̶H̶T̶ ̶I̶H̶T̶ ̶I̶H̶T̶ ̶I̶H̶T̶ ̶I̶H̶T̶ ̶I̶H̶T̶ ̶I̶H̶T̶ ̶I̶H̶T̶ ̶I̶H̶T̶ ̶I̶H̶T̶ ̶I̶H̶T̶ ̶I̶H̶T̶ ̶I̶H̶T̶ ̶I̶H̶T̶
̶I̶H̶T̶ ̶I̶H̶T̶ ̶I̶H̶T̶ ̶I̶H̶T̶ ̶I̶H̶T̶ ̶I̶H̶T̶ ̶I̶H̶T̶ ̶I̶H̶T̶ ̶I̶H̶T̶ ̶I̶H̶T̶ ̶I̶H̶T̶ ̶I̶H̶T̶
̶I̶H̶T̶ ̶I̶H̶T̶ ̶I̶H̶T̶ ̶I̶H̶T̶ ̶I̶H̶T̶ ̶I̶H̶T̶ ̶I̶H̶T̶ ̶I̶H̶T̶ ̶I̶H̶T̶ ̶I̶H̶T̶ ̶I̶H̶T̶ ̶I̶H̶T̶ ̶I̶H̶T̶ //

Contacts: ̶I̶H̶T̶ ̶I̶H̶T̶ ̶I̶H̶T̶ ̶I̶H̶T̶ ̶I̶H̶T̶ ̶I̶H̶T̶ ̶I̶H̶T̶ ̶I̶H̶T̶ ̶I̶H̶T̶ ̶I̶H̶T̶ ̶I̶H̶T̶ ̶I̶H̶T̶
̶I̶H̶T̶ ̶I̶H̶T̶ ̶I̶H̶T̶ ̶I̶H̶T̶ ̶I̶H̶T̶ ̶I̶H̶T̶ ̶I̶H̶T̶ ̶I̶H̶T̶ ̶I̶H̶T̶ ̶I̶H̶T̶ ̶I̶H̶T̶ ̶I̶H̶T̶ ̶I̶H̶T̶ ̶I̶H̶T̶ ///

Follow-up Appointments: ̶I̶H̶T̶ ̶I̶H̶T̶ ̶I̶H̶T̶

New Accounts: //

Overcoming Fear of Failure

Many of us have been raised to be so afraid of failure that we drive through life with our brakes on. Not only is this exhausting, it keeps us from reaching our fullest potential. What is "failure," and why are we so afraid of it?

For most of us, failure means not living up to somebody's expectations of us and being rejected as a result. In the financial services business, that means the more conscientious we are, the more we will "fail" and be rejected. That's terrible! Or is it?

One of the best lecturers on the corporate motivational circuit is Art Mortell. He likes to point out that failure is the only reason that we ever try something new. As long as what we've been doing works even a little bit, we will continue rather than risk trying something new that could be even better. In a word, we need to fail if we are to ultimately succeed.

We're all familiar with Thomas Edison's invention of the electric light bulb. However, did you realize that he failed 10,000 times before he finally found a filament that would last and was economical as well? When asked how he felt about failing 9,000 times (he still hadn't "succeeded" yet), Edison answered that he hadn't failed at all. He had succeeded in finding 9,000 ways that didn't work.

Another great "failure" was Henry J. Kaiser. In his later life, he stated that he had failed at 75 percent of the things he had put his hand to. However, because he was willing to risk, and lost 75 percent of the time, he accomplished staggering tasks. Here are a few of them:

- During World War II, he built 1,500 merchant ships.
- His mills produced over 1 million tons of steel and 20 million pounds of magnesium.
- He was the world's largest producer of cement and the third-largest producer of aluminum.
- He helped build the Hoover and Grand Coulee dams.
- He played a major role in building the San Francisco–Oakland Bay Bridge.

Just imagine what Kaiser would have accomplished if he had never failed at all. Nothing!

Sir Winston Churchill, one of the greatest leaders of all time, gave the shortest speech of his political career when he left Parliament for the last time. Yet it summarized the philosophy he exemplified in overcoming the near-impossible odds against Britain during World War II. It was just seven words long: **"Never give up! Never, never give up!"**

If the average FC obtains 10 good contacts and 1 new account from every 200 prospecting dials, and if the new account results in a first sale with an average commission of $200, then that means that every time you pick up the telephone and dial a prospect, you are earning a dollar. This is true whether the prospect accepts or rejects you, whether the line is busy or the phone goes unanswered. No matter how the call ends, every dial is worth a dollar. How many dials can you make in an hour? As you improve, your level of "success" will increase and the value of each call will increase with it. (*Note:* The actual statistics will vary according to products that your company sells and your experience. The above figures have been true for even the most inexperienced FCs.) Experience can improve the figures more.

Essentially, every time you call a prospect, you succeed! You may succeed in opening a new account, or you may succeed in eliminating a nonstarter from your list, or you may succeed in improving your prospecting approach. But you always succeed! The only way to fail is to fail to try.

YOU ONLY HAVE TO TRY TO SUCCEED!

Time Management

One of the greatest sources of both stress and failure for new FCs is loss of control over the events and information upon which they depend. (Managing stress will be dealt with in more detail in Section Eight.) In fact, studies have shown that the average FC wastes between 40 and 50 percent of each working day. No wonder financial consultants feel stressed!

If you are feeling overwhelmed, there's a good chance that you can accomplish twice as much, and pay yourself twice as much, by learning how to manage your time.

Your first step must be to establish motivating goals for yourself (see Chapter 3). Next, draw up a daily plan that includes all the activities required to attain your goals. It has been said that "if you fail to plan, you plan to fail." We agree. Every successful person makes a plan and works from it to achieve his or her goals.

Remember the man on the mountain? While he didn't fall there, you can be sure he didn't just wish himself there either. When Sir Edmund Hillary climbed Mount Everest, he had a detailed plan of the routes he would take, the equipment he would need, even how far he should travel each day so that he wouldn't exhaust himself. Your goals are your Mount Everest, and you can achieve them if you establish and follow an effective plan.

As long as we are using the analogy of mountain climbing, let's carry it one step further. Hillary didn't just look at a map of the world one day, decide that it would be fun to climb Mount Everest, and quickly develop a plan to do so. He already had experience as a climber. In addition, he spoke to other climbers who had attempted to climb before him to gather information regarding the various routes, techniques that had proved effective or ineffective, and the additional skills that he would need to develop to enable him to reach the summit. Then he developed his plan and practiced the necessary skills to prepare for his ascent.

PLAN YOUR WORK AND WORK YOUR PLAN!

Develop Time-Oriented Skills

One way to improve your record is to handle each piece of paper that crosses your desk only once. Every day you face a mound of papers. Constantly reshuffling them is a great time stealer.

You should also avoid people who want to socialize in the office. Be polite, but firm. Every time someone interrupts what you are doing, that person is stealing not only your time, but also your momentum. Tell him or her that you'd love to talk, but you'd rather do it over lunch. Then wait until lunch. Have your secretary or sales assistant screen your calls and return them during a "return call period" that you have scheduled into your day. When clients come in without an appointment, encourage them to make an appointment to discuss their needs in greater detail after the market has closed. Remember that you are a professional. Do you just "drop in" on your lawyer and expect him to stop what he's doing to see you? Once your clients perceive you as a professional, they will treat you as one.

Make sure you develop good working habits. Most habits require about twenty-one straight days to establish. But once they are there, they can be your most powerful ally in the battle for success. It was once written:

I am your constant companion. In am your greatest helper or heaviest burden.

I will push you onward or drag you down to failure. I am completely at your command.

Half the things you to you might just as well turn over to me and I will do them—quickly and correctly.

I am easily managed—you must merely be firm with me. Show me exactly how you want something done and, after a few lessons, I will do it automatically.

I am the servant of all great people; and, alas, of all failures as well.

Those who are great, I have made great. Those who are failures, I have made failures.

I am not a machine, though I work with all the precision of a machine, plus the intelligence of a person.

You may run me for profit or run me for ruin—it makes no difference to me.

Take me, train me, be firm with me, and I will place the world at your feet.

Be easy with me and I will destroy you.

Who am I? **I AM HABIT!**

Anonymous

> **MAKE A HABIT OF WINNING BY MAKING WINNING HABITS!**

By completing whatever training program your firm offers, you acquired certain skills and knowledge that will be critical to your success as an FC. By reading this book, you are taking another step, seeking additional knowledge about skills that can help you succeed. Seek out successful FCs who have the kind of *character* and the type of business that you admire and find out how they do what they do. Then develop your own plan.

Setting Priorities

As an FC, you have so many tasks and so much information that demands your time and attention that you must establish priorities or you will risk exhausting your resources on the unimportant while neglecting the critical. This is well illustrated by the story of Charles Schwab, the president of Bethlehem Steel Company, and Ivy Lee, a management consultant and efficiency expert.

Ivy Lee had approached Charles Schwab to outline his firm's services. When Lee finished, he told Schwab that by using his services Schwab would know how *to manage better*.

Schwab was outraged and replied that he didn't have time to manage as well as he knew how now. What he wanted in his company was more "doing," *not* "knowing." Schwab told Lee that if he could demonstrate a way to help his managers do the things that they already knew they ought to be doing, he would not only listen, but would pay any reasonable price for the advice.

Lee accepted the challenge and said, "I can give you something in twenty minutes that will step up your "doing" by at least 50 percent." Schwab accepted the challenge.

Lee pulled out a blank three-by-five card and handed it to Schwab with the following directions: "Write on the sheet the six most important tasks that you have to do tomorrow. When that is done, number them in order of importance. Carry this sheet with you and, the first thing tomorrow morning, review item one and begin working on it. Look at item one on the sheet every fifteen minutes until it is completed. Then move on to item two and handle it the same way. Then go on to three, four, et cetera, until you've completed all of your tasks, or until quitting time. Don't worry if you don't finish every item on your list. You'll be working on the most important ones. The others can wait. If you can't finish them all using this method, you can't by using any other method either. In addition, without following some system, you might not have even decided which tasks were most important to begin with.

"Use the last five minutes of each day to plan the next day by making out a "must do" list for tomorrow's tasks. After you've convinced yourself of the value of this system, have your managers try it. When you've given it a thorough trial, send me a check for what *you* think it's worth."

The entire interview lasted only twenty-five minutes. Two weeks later, Schwab sent Lee a check for $25,000 (which is

$1,000 a minute). In today's dollars, Lee would have been paid over $250,000. In five years, this method turned Bethlehem Steel into the biggest independent steel producer in the world and made Schwab a fortune of $100 million.

Today a similar and popular technique is used to set priorities. Write down your tasks and label them "A," "B," or "C."

"A" priorities are the *must do* tasks. They are absolutely critical for success in attaining your goal (if not for survival itself). "B" priorities are important, *should do* tasks, but if you don't get them done today, there is no immediate threat. "C" priorities are tasks it would be nice to accomplish today, but it wouldn't much matter if you didn't.

Unfortunately, too many of us tend to focus on the "C" tasks first. Because they are unimportant, they are rarely threatening. Also, they frequently take little time, so we look to get them out of the way in order to focus our full attention on the "A" tasks. This rationalization has resulted in failure more than almost any other. No "B" priority should be touched until every "A" priority has been accomplished (or cannot be worked on at that time), and no "C" priority should be touched as long as any "A" or "B" priority is unfinished. Since 80 percent of priorities are "Cs," this rule can save you a great deal of time.

Once you have established your "A," "B," and "C" priorities, number them according to importance within each category. Now put them into a daily plan.

Daily Plans

Just as you establish goals for your life, you need a plan to accomplish each day's tasks. End each day by writing down a plan for the next. Include everything that you need to get done the next day (appointments, calls, etc.) and prioritize them. Then, when you get to the office, you'll be ready to start right to work. Exhibit 4-1 presents a typical example.

Remember that the purpose of prioritizing is to focus your attention and energy on accomplishing the most important things

EXHIBIT 4-1

A3: Cold-call 100 prospects.
A2: Phone list of "follow-up calls."
A1: Phone list of clients for XYZ product.
B1: See sales manager *re* new sales assistant.
A4: 5:00 P.M. appointment with Mr. Jones *re* new acct.
B2: Read prospectus on XYZ mutual fund for Thursday's sales
      meeting.
C2: Read lesson 6 on the economy for fin. plan. course.
C1: Update files.

each day. If you don't complete every task, let it be the unimportant ones you miss.

Establish a Work Schedule

Set up a daily schedule and establish blocks of time for specific activities, such as cold calling, making follow-up calls, phoning clients to make a sale, planning and preparation, appointments, and paperwork. Once you have developed your schedule, post it and commit yourself to following it. Exhibit 4-2 is one such schedule.

EXHIBIT 4-2
Daily Schedule

7:00–9:00 A.M.	Cold-call business executives at their offices.
9:00–9:30 A.M.	Listen to closed-circuit broadcast of strategy.
9:30–10:00 A.M.	Review any new financial information (e.g., *Wall Street Journal,* in-house news service).
10:00–12:00 noon	Call clients with sales idea.
12:00–1:00 P.M.	Take lunch.
1:00–2:00 P.M.	Return morning phone calls. Contact operations *re* follow-up on account problems.
2:00–4:00 P.M.	Cold-call.
4:00–5:00 P.M.	Update paperwork (e.g., new account forms, mailings).
5:00–6:30 P.M.	See appointments.
6:30–7:30 P.M.	Take dinner.
7:30–8:50 P.M.	Cold call.
8:50–9:10 P.M.	Plan and prepare for tomorrow.

Exhibit 4-2 is just an example. A new broker with few or no clients should substitute cold calling for calling clients.

Summary

- List your goals and set your priorities.
- Make a daily "To Do" list.
- Start with "A" priorities, not with "C's."
- Ask yourself: What is the best use of my time *right now?*
- Handle each piece of paper just once. You don't have time to sort through information several times.
- Spend a few minutes at the end of each day reviewing today's activities and planning tomorrow's.
- **DO IT NOW!**

COMMUNICATION SKILLS

The art of selling is the art of communicating, of convincing others of your point of view. Indeed, you could say that the best test of your effectiveness is whether or not your listeners change their behavior or point of view as you desire. If you can't convince your client to buy, you're out of business.

To an extent, you might say that we are all salespeople in some way, and all our listeners are our clients or customers. For that reason, the word *client* will be used throughout this book to represent your listener, whether that person be a customer, a subordinate, an associate, a peer, or a superior. After all, we have to "sell" our bosses as well as our customers on our ideas if we are to get anything accomplished. The same could also be said of our friends and family.

Many people feel threatened by salespeople. Once they perceive you as a salesperson, they will avoid you. Why? The last time you went into a store to buy something, what did you say to the sales clerk who asked if he or she could help you? If you're like most of us, you probably said, "No, thank you. I'm just looking." This reply voices instant sales resistance! Even though you went into the store with the intention of buying something, the minute someone offered to sell it to you, you backed away.

Why? Because most of us have an unconscious image of sales-persons as interested only in our money and not in us. We may even feel that they see us as objects to be used or manipulated to obtain their end—sales.

This resentment at being viewed as an object rather than a person may well be the reason that more and more professionals are taking a client-centered approach to selling financial services. In this approach, we treat the client as a person with financial needs that we, the professionals, are here to meet. Our experi-ence has been that clients respond with loyalty in good *and* bad markets. In addition, because we are perceived as resources to help solve problems instead of as adversaries who cause prob-lems, clients are more open to sales ideas and are freer with referrals.

There are only two ways to increase your income: (1) obtain more clients, and (2) earn more commissions from the clients you currently service. The whole idea of client-centered sales is to put the client's needs first and the sale second. Profes-sionals who try this approach tell us that they end up gathering much more of their clients' assets to manage, and hence make far more sales. They also receive more referrals, thereby increasing the number of clients they service. The key is to find out what your client really needs and then work *with* him or her to sup-ply it.

We all like people who listen to us. Yet the biggest com-plaint against financial consultants is that they only call to sell. Most of us rarely take the time to really hear what our clients are telling us. *We* know what's best for them. Think about this:

If you spoke excellent German, and had a client who was from Germany but spoke fair English, you would undoubtedly speak to him in German. Why? Because:

1. It would improve the chances that he would understand what you intended to say.
2. It would show that you cared enough about him to try to communicate in his language.

Just as we all have our own way of looking at things, so do we all have our own "private language." You will be effective to the extent that you recognize and communicate from your client's point of view and in his or her language.

Remember the sign that says:

> I KNOW YOU THINK YOU UNDERSTAND WHAT YOU THOUGHT I SAID, BUT I'M NOT SURE THAT YOU REALIZE THAT WHAT YOU HEARD IS NOT WHAT I MEANT.

The purpose of this book is to help you increase sales and retain your clients in good and bad markets by working from the *client's* point of view.

Client-Centered Selling

Effective communication is the financial consultant's life-blood. To be effective, you must overcome the barriers to communication. Only then can you convey your genuine interest to your client. In the paragraphs that follow, we will demonstrate ways to communicate a caring mind-set, as well as how to deal with the roadblocks to understanding.

In the marketing of ideas as well as products, marketing professionals look for individuals they call "key communicators" or centers of influence. Essentially, these people are the trendsetters and opinion formers of their groups. Once they become sold on an idea or a product, the rest of the group tends to follow their lead. Most advertising, whether economic, political, or social, is directed at those key communicators because advertisers know the effect that they will have upon the other members of their group.

As a professional financial services adviser, you are the key communicator for financial services. You know your product line and understand how your products will help meet your clients' needs. Thus you have considerable impact upon your clients' opinions regarding the quality of products and their need to purchase them.

A Caring Mind Set

One of the most important factors in communications is the mind-set of the individuals involved. Your mind-set, or attitude, about your business, yourself, and your clients is communicated clearly to those with whom you deal. When you meet a client, the first impression you make creates a mental image of you that will strongly influence that client's expectations of you in the relationship.

Books such as *Megatrends* and *In Search of Excellence* have emphasized that to be successful in sales, you must put the customer first and the sale second. **This is the key to client-centered selling.**

**THE KEY TO CLIENT-CENTERED SELLING
IS A CARING MIND-SET.**

We all know how important first impressions are. Once set, they frequently stay with us for the rest of the relationship. Unfortunately, bad first impressions have a way of ending even the most potentially profitable relationships before they begin. It has been suggested that an initial impression—good or bad—is made within the first three seconds.

When you meet a client for the first time, what you are wearing and everything you do and say (or fail to do or say) communicate important information about your attitudes and mind-set. This, in turn, establishes a mind-set in the client. Whether or not this is a fair way to judge someone is immaterial. How we look, talk, and act all contribute to the client's feeling that we are or are not like him or her.

**YOU ONLY GET ONE CHANCE TO MAKE
A FIRST IMPRESSION!**

Fortunately, we can "package" ourselves to create the image we want to project initially. This package provides the first opportunity to unconsciously influence others (those interested should see John T. Malloy's, *New Dress for Success*). The next opportunity to positively influence a person occurs when we begin to communicate.

While most people feel that they can be very effective in person, many of your initial contacts as an FC will be made over the phone. All that you are and all that you hope to be to this individual must therefore be communicated in your voice. What you say and the way you say it will establish for the client whether you are just another sales person or a Professional Financial Consultant.

Barriers to Effective Communication

It's hard enough to build a relationship and make a sale without having to deal with interference. Yet barriers constantly appear to disturb our efforts. Some are beyond our control, but we create most of them ourselves.

Many things can hinder your ability to communicate with a client. Whether they are external or internal, you must be aware of them and take whatever steps are necessary to minimize them.

External Barriers

The three most common external barriers are:

1. Interruptions by someone in the office, your sales assistant, or your phone.
2. The general noise level in the office.
3. Visual distractions such as the Quotron, a computer, the view out the window, or the actions of other people in the office.

MINIMIZE EXTERNAL DISTRACTIONS.

Internal Barriers

The internal barriers that we build up to one extent or another are numerous. These include:

1. Anxiety/fear of failure. This can be very destructive to clear communication because it comes across in your voice and can distract your client. Do you want the client to wonder why you are anxious? ("Is there something wrong with what he wants me to buy?")
2. Family problems/worrying about personal or office problems.
3. Attitude barriers, such as disrespect for the client, and prejudices (the client's or yours).
4. Worrying about your needs instead of the client's.
5. Cultural/customs differences.
6. Accents and speech patterns, such as speed and slang. (*Note:* People generally listen at about the same speed that they speak, and nothing is more common than the image of the "fast-talking salesman.")
7. Emotions such as anger or depression.
8. Physical discomfort such as hunger or stiffness from sitting too long.
9. Interrupting people or "mind reading"; thinking about your response instead of listening to what the other person is saying.
10. Daydreaming while the client is talking.
11. Letting your own ignorance lead you to ramble.
12. Jargon or slang. Remember how you feel when a doctor or lawyer uses jargon when speaking to you, or when someone uses slang with which you are unfamiliar. Your client will probably feel the same say. Jargon and slang hurt relationships.

People want to be understood and to understand what you are

telling them. Jargon and slang can cause potentially disastrous misunderstandings.

EXAMPLE—THE "W.C.": An English lady visiting Switzerland decided to make that country her permanent residence. She asked the local schoolmaster to help her locate a suitable room. When she found a place that fit her specifications, she returned to England for her baggage. After arriving home, she suddenly realized that she had not seen a "W.C." (a British slang term that stands for "water closet" or "toilet") in the apartment, so she promptly wrote the schoolmaster concerning the matter. Here is the letter that she wrote:

Mrs. J. William Barnes
11 Charringcross Road
London, England
23 June 1958

Master Wilhelm Schmidt
226 Shubert Strasse
Jolingen, Switzerland

Dear Sir,

     During my recent trip to your country, I was so enchanted that I decided to make the lovely apartment that you showed me my permanent home. However, when I returned to London, I remembered that I had not seen a W.C., and was concerned about the accommodations.

     Please write to me as soon as you can to reassure me on this matter.

Yours very truly,

The teacher, being unfamiliar with British slang, was completely puzzled by the initials "W.C.," so he asked the parish priest to help him with the problem. Together the two men decided that the only possible thing "W.C." could stand for was "Wayside Chapel." The schoolmaster then wrote the lady this letter:

Master Wilhelm Schmidt
226 Shubert Strasse
Jolingen, Switzerland
2 July 1958

Mrs. J. William Barnes
11 Charringcross Road
London, England

Dear Madam,

I am proud to inform you that the W.C. is located only nine miles from the house, and is situated in a beautiful grove of trees. It is capable of holding 350 people at a time, and is open on Tuesday, Thursday, and Sunday of each week. A large number of people are expected during the summer months, so it is suggested that you go early, although there is plenty of standing room.

Some people like to bring lunch and make a day of it. I would especially recommend that you attend Thursdays, when there is organ accompaniment. The acoustics are excellent—even the most delicate sounds can be heard.

It may be of interest to you to know that my daughter was married in the W.C.; and that's where she met her husband. I can still remember that wondrous day; there were ten to a seat, usually occupied by one. It was wonderful to see the expressions on their faces.

Plans are being made to have a bazaar in the W.C. The proceeds will be used to provide plush seats. My wife is quite delicate, thus, she cannot attend regularly. It has been almost a year since she went last. Naturally, it pains her very much not to be able to attend more often.

The W.C. holds a great position in the hearts of all those of our community. I am sure that it will become as much a part of your life as it is of ours. I have every wish to accommodate you in every possible way. If you write again soon, I am sure that I can reserve a seat for you, either up front or near the door, whichever you prefer. If I can be of further service, please do not hesitate to ask.

Sincerely yours,
The Schoolmaster

It should be obvious from this example how easily the use of slang can confuse communication and hurt a relationship. Professional jargon (e.g., the P/E ratio of a stock) can be just as damaging as slang.

SLANG/JARGON IS LIKE A FOREIGN LANGUAGE: CUSTOMERS WHO AREN'T FAMILIAR WITH IT MAY FEEL LIKE OUTSIDERS.

CHAPTER 6

Perfecting Verbal Skills

We have all had the experience of speaking to someone and suddenly realizing that our listener has mentally drifted away. Effective communication is a two-way street. If we want to maintain someone's attention, we must give him or her a relevant benefit for listening to us. In turn, we must demonstrate that we are listening.

It requires a great deal more than an occasional "uh huh" or a nod of the head to communicate that you are listening. You must let clients know that you understand what they are saying and how they feel. While it is tempting to simply say, "I understand," especially in response to an objection or a question, no one will believe that you do understand until you demonstrate it.

Below is a review of several simple, yet essential, communication skills that will help you both gain the information you need to understand what someone is telling you and demonstrate your understanding. No attempt has been made to be comprehensive because these skills are commonly taught in communications courses. We present them here only for review purposes and to define some of the "jargon" that we will be using throughout the book.

Probing

Asking questions, or "probing," is a very effective way to obtain information from clients about their needs, interests, and objections. Many people feel threatened when they are asked questions, however, because they believe the inquirer is intruding upon their privacy. Even so, research has shown that **people will answer virtually *any* question if given a convincing rationale for doing so.** If you doubt this, think back to the last time you had a physical exam. Try to remember some of the extremely personal questions you answered simply because the doctor needed the information to keep you healthy. That is why it is important to *always* give the client a reason for answering your questions.

EXAMPLE: You might preface your questions with a statement that lets clients know that your purpose is to help them to the best of your ability, and that, consequently, you need to ask a few questions to make sure that you understand exactly what they need.

> *FC:* Our company has hundreds of products and services to meet our customers' needs. Needless to say, not every product or service is helpful to every customer. In order to help me to offer only ideas that would be appropriate for you, would you mind if I asked you a few questions to determine the nature of your needs?

Probing skills are particularly helpful when used in conjunction with the psychological profiling and rapport-building techniques that you will learn in Sections Three and Four. In addition, a combination of open and closed probes will allow you to conduct easy sales interviews and to make more powerful presentations.

Closed Probes

Closed probes are questions that require either yes/no or short answers. For example: "Where do you live?" or "Are your financial objectives in the nature of growth of capital, income, or total return?'' These questions serve a variety of purposes, since they:

- Elicit specific information: "How many children do you have?"
- Verify and/or confirm: "Do you mean that you . . . ?"
- Can be in the form of either/or: "Would you prefer ordinary term or whole life insurance?"
- Elicit commitment: "Will you be able to deliver the bonds by settlement date?"

(*Note:* Because closed probes tend to be very controlling, using more than two in a row may seem like an interrogation and make the client defensive.)

Open Probes

Open probes are questions that require longer answers. They are generally used to gather considerable amounts of information. They involve the client more deeply in the conversation and often begin with such words as "how" or "what." They:

- Encourage people to talk: "What do you like best about your current broker, Ms. Jones?"
- Gain more information: "What steps have you already taken to achieve your retirement goals, Mr. Smith?"
- Build rapport: "Tell me about yourself."
- Uncover feelings: "How do you feel about the current market?"
- Keep the conversation going: "Tell me more."
- Can disarm hostility (see "CLAPping," in the next chapter).
- Direct the conversation more subtly: "Let's talk more about . . ."

(*Note:* Ask only one question at a time, and remember that every statement should be followed by a probe for acceptance of what you are saying.)

Summary Probes

Summary probes are special types of closed probes that are used to determine if you are "on track" with the client. They consist of summarizing in the form of a question, what has just been discussed. For example: "Am I correct in understanding that your chief concern is guaranteeing your children's education?" or "Let me summarize what we've gotten so far. . . . Is that right?" Summary probes:

• Demonstrate your interest to the client.
• Show that you are listening and trying to understand the client's point of view.
• Let both you and the client know whether you have understood the client correctly.

> **USE PROBES TO DEMONSTRATE INTEREST AND TO ELICIT INFORMATION.**

Silence

Silence can be very effective in eliciting a response from a client. Virtually everyone becomes uncomfortable during a prolonged silence in a conversation and desires to fill the gap. As a result, this kind of probe is particularly apt with clients who tend to chatter. It should be apparent, however, that silence can only be an effective probe if you have the self-discipline to maintain it in the face of your own discomfort. Use silence carefully and rarely. It is best employed in "closing" situations as a way of forcing the issue.

Acknowledging

In order to effectively establish rapport, it is critical to communicate to people that you recognize and *understand* how they feel. If you fail to do this, you will give people the impression that you are more concerned with your own agenda than with theirs. This makes them feel manipulated and builds great barriers against forming a worthwhile business relationship.

An effective way to acknowledge how someone feels is to paraphrase what that person has said with a summary probe: "Mrs. Brown, it sounds as though your last experience with a broker was not a happy one. Is that right?" Remember, acknowledging a client's feeling or concern is *not* the same as agreeing with it.

WE ALL NEED TO FEEL ACKNOWLEDGED.

Bridging

Have you ever been engaged in a conversation with someone and had no idea what the other person was referring to? *Bridging* consists of tying a previous conversation, an earlier part of the present conversation, or a new concept to the topic currently being discussed. It is also an effective technique for steering a rambling conversation back on track (e.g., "That reminds me of what we were talking about earlier" or "The last time we spoke, you said . . ."). The most common use of bridging is in the "benefit opener" of a sales call (e.g., "Ms. Jones, the last time we spoke, you indicated that your primary investment concern was tax-free income. Is that still the case?").

BRIDGING KEEPS THE DISCUSSION CONNECTED.

Building

Building is a skill that allows the client to sell *himself* on *your* idea. It consists of three steps. When the client makes a positive statement about something you are discussing:

1. Reinforce it.
2. Add a comment extending what the client has said.
3. Verify the client's acceptance.

For example:

Client: One of the things that I like best about a municipal investment trust is the tax-free income.

FC: You're right! The municipal investment trust does provide tax-free income, *and* it pays monthly! Don't you agree?

Restating the client's comment reinforces what he said.

> **BUILDING BUILDS MOMENTUM.**

Analogy

Some of the most frustrating moments for a FC occur when trying to explain unfamiliar new programs and concepts to clients in ways they can understand. One helpful technique is to draw analogies from clients' own experiences.

An analogy is a comparison between two concepts, one familiar to the client and the other strange. The following passage is a typical example of how an FC uses analogy to illuminate a new concept for a client:

FC: Jim, I think you once told me that you are a scoutmaster for your local troop. As such, one of the things that you teach the boys is to always be prepared. In today's roller-coaster market, buying a put to protect your stock can help you to always "be prepared."

> **ANALOGIES MAKE THE COMPLEX SIMPLE.**

Summary

The verbal skills that we have just reviewed are powerful communications tools. While many financial consultants are intellectually aware of them, the "stars" use verbal skills consistently. Conscious practice of the verbal skills using the Ben Franklin approach mentioned in Chapter 1 will help make these skills enduring habits.

Responding to Clients' Concerns

Clients can become concerned or resistant for many reasons. One of the most common is their perception of a financial consultant as someone who is more interested in making the sale than in helping them meet their needs. Once this impression has been formed, needless resistance is created and the sale becomes much more difficult.

We have found that **the easiest way to overcome a client's resistance to your idea is to avoid creating the resistance in the first place.** You can prevent resistance by following two important steps:

1. Establish that you are a source of support or an ally in the client's efforts to meet his or her needs.
2. ''Presell'' your ideas in terms of the client's needs.

(*Note:* A powerful way to avoid resistance is to adopt your client's model of the world. Then the client will perceive you as being ''just like me.'' This technique will be covered in detail in Sections Three and Four).

Unfortunately, no matter how well prepared you are, you

will at times encounter client resistance to what you want to achieve. This may occur for any of several reasons:

1. Many financial consultants have a tendency to deviate from the subject of how their product or service will benefit the client.
2. FCs are sometimes insensitive to the client's concerns as communicated during the conversation.
3. The client has previously heard something negative about the FC's company or product, or has had a negative experience with a similar product in the past.
4. The client may have already committed funds elsewhere.
5. The client suffers from inertia, or the tendency to avoid taking action.

Let's look at an example of a conversation in which the client's initial concern/resistance was *not* acknowledged. The FC has just presented the concept of purchasing a long-term fixed-income investment such as a bond. Notice how the conversation deteriorates:

> *Client:* I'm not too sure that this is the right investment for me. I hear that inflation is expected to go up again.
>
> *FC:* Don't worry about it. Now is the right time to be holding long-term investments. These bonds are just the right thing for you at this moment in time.
>
> *Client:* I'm still uncomfortable with the idea.
>
> *FC:* I've really thought about your situation carefully and I am convinced that this is the right investment for you.
>
> *Client:* Let me think about it.
>
> *FC:* What's there to think about?
>
> *Client:* I'll call you when I've made up my mind.

You can see how the FC's failure to acknowledge and deal with the client's concern hardened the client's resistance. The FC didn't even bother to determine the nature of the concern. We'll discover more about this client's concerns as we continue the example below.

CLAPing: Four Key Steps to Overcoming Resistance

Whenever a client begins to resist you, it is important to drop your agenda for a while in order to determine what is causing the client to resist. Failure to do this inevitably increases the resistance and, at best, results in a breakdown in the conversation. At worst, it results in the loss of the relationship.

To overcome resistance, there are four easy steps you should take before attempting to respond to the client's position. Only after these steps have been followed can you respond to the client's concern and, if appropriate, return to your agenda. The four key steps, known as CLAP, are:

1. **C**larify
2. **L**egitimize
3. **A**cknowledge
4. **P**robe

Step 1: Clarify

First of all, you must be sure that you are dealing with the real source of the client's concern. It is all too easy to respond to what you *think* the client's apprehensions are, but if you do this, you may end up dealing with something other than the real problem. This might happen in either of two ways:

1. Sometimes a client resists because he or she is uncomfortable with an aspect of your presentation without being entirely sure why (the client may wish additional information, feel that you are being "too pushy," or not understand some of the technical jargon being used). In such cases, it is important to patiently help the client explore the cause of his or her discomfort until it is clearly identified so that you can usefully discuss it. Attempting to overcome the resistance without identifying its cause invariably leads to resentment on the client's part.

2. Sometimes the real cause of the discomfort is not the one the client first gives (e.g., the client may claim to be uninterested in an idea when, in reality, he is too embarrassed to admit that

he hasn't taken the time to read the report you sent him). For this reason, it is very important to persist in your efforts to *clarify* and not to quit until *all* of the causes of the client's resistance have been uncovered and dealt with. Let's go back to our earlier example.

> *Client:* I'm not sure that this is the right investment for me. I hear that inflation is expected to go up again.
>
> *FC:* [*Probing*] Are there any other areas of concern for you?
>
> *Client:* Not really. I'm just worried about inflation.
>
> *FC:* [*Clarifying*] So, your primary concern is the potential rise in inflation and the impact that that might have on this kind of investment. Is that right?
>
> *Client:* Sure, because I want to make sure that what I'm trying to accomplish with my investments isn't offset by inflation.
>
> *FC:* In other words, you want to maintain your current lifestyle when you retire, right?
>
> *Client:* Absolutely! I want to be able to continue to live in comfort.

By clarifying, you are verifying that you have correctly understood the client's concern.

Once you have *clarified* the nature of the resistance, you must communicate to the client that you not only *acknowledge* and understand his concern, but also accept it as *legitimate* (a client's concerns are *always* legitimate, even when unfounded). *Remember:* Failure to convey that you regard a client's question or concern as legitimate is equivalent to telling the client that you don't consider it (or him) to be very important.

Steps 2 and 3: Legitimize and Acknowledge

When clients resist committing to what we want, it is frequently because they have concerns, or *anxieties,* that our presentation hasn't relieved. Unfortunately, before we can respond to a client's objections, we must successfully communicate to him that we understand his concerns and that it is all right for him to be open about them (i.e., that we are not threatened by his resistance). We'll continue our previous example:

FC: Your concern about inflation, and its potential effect upon your retirement, is understandable. In fact, I wish more of my clients were as aware of inflation. Because the risk of inflation will always be present to some extent, I've incorporated an inflationary hedge into the fixed-income investment we're discussing. This should provide you with the best of both worlds. Would you like me to give you the details?

(*Note:* Legitimizing and acknowledging a client's concerns does not mean that you agree with them, only that you respect and understand them. Many FCs *tell* clients that they understand their concerns but fail to demonstrate that understanding. Therefore, they often appear condescending and defensive and cause the client to become resistant. Always remember that as a professional, you will *never* need to be defensive because you will *always* do the best possible job for your clients. Hence, if a client resists or becomes upset, it won't be because of your performance.)

Step 4: Probe

Having communicated your understanding and acceptance of the client's concern, you must *probe* to determine if your assessment is accurate. This step accomplishes two things:

1. It demonstrates your interest to the client.
2. If you find out that you are on the wrong track, you will be able to go back and try again until your assessment is confirmed by the client. This will prevent the frustration that comes from trying to solve the wrong problem. Most clients will appreciate your efforts to understand them and be willing to try again.

If you are correct in your assessment of the problem, you not only improve your level of rapport with your client, but also lower the client's resistance. In addition, you know that you are on the right track in meeting the client's needs. Even if the nature of the concern is such that you cannot complete your presentation at the first meeting, you have at least improved your relationship with the client and paved the way for your next meeting.

Paraphrasing

Perhaps the easiest way to CLAP is through the use of *paraphrasing*. When the client states a concern, paraphrase that concern in your own words and probe to see if you are correct (this is effectively the same thing as using a *summary probe*). In so doing, you simultaneously *clarify* the nature of the client's concern, *acknowledge* and *legitimize* it, and demonstrate your understanding—or at least your desire to understand—and verify the correctness of your assessment.

EXAMPLE:

Client: This market looks so shaky that I'm not sure I want to risk investing in stocks right now.

FC: Bill, it sounds as if you are worried about the safety of your investments. Is that right?

Once you have demonstrated your understanding, it is safe to tell the client that you understand. After that you should respond to the concern.

Responding

Having successfully determined the nature of the client's resistance, you must now respond to it. Overly long answers tend to be given by individuals who are nervous and unsure of themselves, so remember the KISS principle: Keep it short and sweet. If you appear nervous or defensive, the client may wonder what you are nervous about and whether you have something to hide. This can quickly undermine the rapport you built through CLAPing.

EXAMPLE: Take the case of the little boy who asked his mother where he came from. His mother became acutely embarrassed and provided a detailed answer that included a complete description of how babies are conceived and born. The boy looked increasingly confused throughout the discussion and his mother became increasingly uncomfortable as her "lecture" progressed.

Finally, when it was over and she "probed" to see if he was satisfied, he said, "Gee, Mom, that's wild! Johnny comes from Chicago."

While you can always expand on an answer if necessary, it is very hard to take back information that confuses your listener or increases his discomfort.

With clients or prospects who are negative, it's important for you to remain positive. Turn potential failures into successes by "reframing" what the client has said into something else you can use.

EXAMPLE:

Client: I don't know about this, Bob. Rukeyser on TV says that the market looks very weak right now.

FC: It sounds as if you're worried that he might be right. Is that it?

Client: Yeah.

FC: I can understand that. I can't tell you what a pleasure it is to finally have a client who is interested enough in his investments to really look into the market and the economy. Bill, you know that our analysts have been highly regarded on Wall Street for years. Would you like me to send you some information on what they think the market will be doing over the next six months?

Client: Sure.

FC: Good. I'll do that right away. Then, after you've had a chance to look over what our experts say, we'll chat again. If you're still uncomfortable with the market, we'll look for alternatives. How does that sound?

Probe Again

Once you have dealt with the client's objections, it is important to probe again to determine, first, if he has understood and accepted your response, and second, if he has any further questions or concerns. Once this has been accomplished, you may return to your agenda and the remainder of your presentation if you feel that it is still appropriate.

EXAMPLE 1:

[Concern.]

Client: Brokers have gotten very bad press coverage lately. How do I know that I can trust you?

[Clarifies with summary probe.]

FC: It sounds as though you are worried about how honest I'll be. Is that right?

Client: Well, yes.

[Legitimizes and acknowledges.]
[Probe also elicits criteria.]

FC: I can understand that. The press has raised doubts about the integrity of the brokerage industry in the minds of many people. I guess it's a little like the bad press doctors get sometimes. A very small number cheat. But that doesn't make all, or even most, doctors dishonest. It's the same with us. Mrs. Jones, what would you need to feel comfortable working with us?

Client: I'd like to see who's handling my money, and what kind of place it is. I can usually tell by someone's face if they're honest.

[Response.]
[Probe.]

FC: It sounds as if you'd like to come into the office to meet me and see how we work. Is that right?

Client: Yes.

[Response.]

[Probe.]

FC: That sounds like a great idea. I like to meet all my clients face-to-face, and this will give us an opportunity to discuss your needs. May I also suggest that you speak to the Better Business Bureau about us? It's your money, and I think that it's important for you to feel comfortable with the people you invest with. Do you have any other concerns or questions?

Client: Not right now.

FC: That's fine. If you think of any more, you can bring them up when we meet.

EXAMPLE 2:

[Concern.]

Client: How long have you been in this business?

[Clarifies with summary probe.]

FC: Mr. Smith, it sounds as though you are concerned with how well I know this business. Is that right?

Client: Yes. If I'm going to turn over large amounts of money to you, I want to be sure that you know what you're doing.

FC: I can understand that. Your money is important to you and you want to know that it will be handled wisely. I'm not going to present myself as an expert on every aspect of this business. That's impossible. But I do know how to handle your day-to-day needs, and should you develop a need beyond my expertise, I will know which expert in our company to call on to handle it. I'll also work with you and that expert to make sure that you understand and are comfortable with his suggestions. How does that sound

[Legitimizes and acknowledges client's concern.]
[Response.]

[Probe.]

Client: Fine.

FC: Great! Do you have any other questions or concerns?

[Probes for additional concerns.]

Summary

Obviously, not all clients' questions will be stalls or objections. When clients ask a simple information-gathering or clarifying question (and you are confident that that is the real purpose behind the question), just give a short factual answer and continue with your presentation. Otherwise, use the CLAPing technique. (*Note:* Appendix 4 contains a list of additional responses to common stalls and objections.) **Remember, objections and questions are not necessarily "bad." They indicate that the client is at least thinking about what you are saying.**)

> **WHEN FACED WITH AN OBJECTION**
> **OR A CONCERN, CLAP.**

IDENTIFYING YOUR CLIENT'S PERSONALITY TYPE

The art of bringing your client to your point of view centers on your ability to "walk in his shoes." Effective communication, rapport-building skills, and the ability to quickly determine a client's psychological makeup are powerful tools in selling. They enable you to step inside your client's world and demonstrate how accepting your idea or program will help him to meet his needs.

> YOU CANNOT *NOT* COMMUNICATE.

In this book, communication includes all the behaviors, feelings, and expectations within a relationship between two people. In sales, as in marriage, it is impossible not to communicate. Unfortunately, the very extensiveness of the information exchanged in any relationship, as well as the expectations that each individual brings to the relationship, can make effective communications very difficult. For example, if your client expects you to try to sell him something simply because you need another commission, he will probably increase his level of resistance, not only to the sale, but also to the relationship itself.

In this section, you will learn techniques that will enable you to psychologically profile clients within the first few minutes of speaking to them. In addition, you will learn ways to respond to clients' emotional needs while talking to them.

===================== CHAPTER 8 =====================

Four Basic Personality Types

Over the years, psychologists have developed a variety of systems to help understand people's actions. As a result, there are many systems available for profiling people's behavior, all the way to psychiatric evaluation. In this book, we provide a simplified system of categorizing the behavior you see in others in order to help you communicate more effectively. This system will also assist you in selecting the sales techniques that best fit your own personal style. This chapter discusses clients' primary behavioral attributes, and then consolidates them into a psychological profiling system.

Before we present the basis of the psychological profiling system, take a moment to think of the people you know, or know of, who fit the following descriptions:

• Bill is always "hanging" out with the crowd." He bases his sense of self-worth on other people's reactions to and perceptions of him. Hence he is eager to please, and may even appear to be a "social butterfly." He is very garrulous, and tends to be quite conscious of the latest fashions and trends.

• Jane always "goes by the book" because "rules were made for good reasons." She rarely takes chances and does not wish to stand out from the crowd. Although she does not want to be a leader, she resents whoever does take the lead. She will frequently gossip about people, but will rarely confront them to their face. If a new idea is suggested, she usually has some reason why it won't work and shouldn't even be attempted.

• Jack is very dogmatic and always has to be right. When he is wrong, he tries to bully his way through, often at the "top of his lungs." He always wants to be in control, and is often contemptuous of others. His three most frequently used words are "I," "me," and "myself."

• Samantha is an independent thinker who is respectful of others' feelings and opinions. First she listens, then she makes up her own mind. A natural leader in any group, she is social, polite, and friendly, but not insincerely so. When necessary, she is able to set limits on herself and others.

Chances are that you know several people who fit quite well into some of these profiles. Actually, most of us demonstrate at least some of the traits of all of these categories at one time or another, but each of us tends to fit one profile better than any of the others.

The purpose of associating your friends and acquaintances with these profiles is to demonstrate how true-to-life psychological profiling can be. The following pages will provide you with additional insights into people you already know as well as people you have yet to meet.

Primary Personality Traits

For present purposes, we have selected two basic personality types, the **Leader** and the **Follower,** and two modifying characteristics, **Hostile** and **Friendly.** These terms—Leader/Follower and Hostile/Friendly—have many more meanings, or connotations, than their dictionary definitions suggest. They imply general orientations regarding how a person deals with other people. Each personality type will be explained in detail on the following pages.

Leader

The Leader has a drive to take control in personal encounters and a desire to be paramount. This may manifest itself in a cluster of traits such as initiative, decisiveness, forcefulness, and independence. The Leader is goal-oriented and self-motivating.

Follower

The Follower has the disposition to let others take the lead and make decisions in personal encounters. This may manifest itself in traits like dependence, indecisiveness, unassertiveness, and passivity. The Follower demonstrates a willingness to be controlled, to avoid personal confrontations, and to comply with other people's wishes. Both goals and motivation must often be imposed on the Follower from the outside.

Friendliness

Friendliness is basically a concern for others. It involves recognition of the value and dignity of other people and a sensitivity to their needs. In fact, friendliness could be defined as the extent to which we are involved with people and are sensitive to their needs. It implies a realization that we can only achieve our goals by helping others (e.g., our clients and co-workers) to achieve theirs. Friendliness has a "win-win" or an "I'm OK, you're OK" orientation.

Hostility

Hostility is a lack of regard for others and a concentration on self. It embodies the attitude that other people matter less than oneself and therefore deserve less care. It implies indifference to others, insensitivity to their needs and ideas, resistance to collaboration, and, in some cases, outright animosity. Hostile people are often emotionally cold, insensitive, and manipulative. They are "self-oriented," and adopt a win-lose, or an "I'm OK, you're *not* OK" stance in their dealings with other people.

The personality that we show others is a combination of the four traits we've just discussed, and can be demonstrated on a grid. Which traits predominate in any given situation are usually determined by the context of that situation. To enable you to understand the grid system that we use in consultative selling, we have divided the traits along two axes in Exhibit 8-1.

EXHIBIT 8-1
___

The vertical line deals with the Leader and Follower traits.

LEADER
      | Decisive, forceful,
      | independent
      |
FOLLOWER
       Indecisive, passive,
       dependent

The horizontal line deals with the Hostility and Friendliness traits.

HOSTILE ——————————— FRIENDLY
 Self-oriented,   Other-oriented,
 insensitive,   sensitive,
 uncooperative   cooperative
___

Now let's merge these traits and see how they provide an easy-to-use psychological profiling system.

Client Traits

In Exhibit 8-2, we have combined the trait lines to show the interrelationship among the primary traits.

The four primary traits of Leader, Follower, Hostile, and Friendly can be paired in various ways. The resulting combinations produce easily recognized common personality types. In the next few pages, we will briefly describe the four types, as well as the client characteristics associated with each.

EXHIBIT 8-2

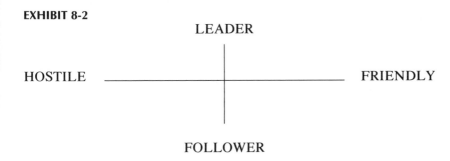

LEADER

HOSTILE ——————————————————— FRIENDLY

FOLLOWER

Socialite

A **Socialite** (Exhibit 8-3) is a "Friendly Follower": someone who is always "hanging out with the crowd." Socialites derive their sense of self-worth from other people's reactions and perceptions of them. Hence they are eager to please and often come across as "social butterflies." They are garrulous and keep up with the latest fashions and trends. Because they tend to subordinate their goals to the desires of the group, Socialites rarely take the initiative. They see the world from a "You're OK, I'm *not* OK" orientation.

EXHIBIT 8-3
Friendly + Follower = Socialite.

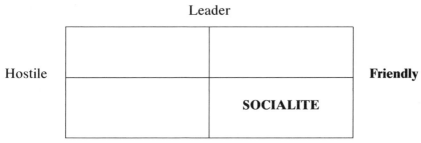

Leader

Hostile **Friendly**

SOCIALITE

Follower

This profile of the Socialite really represents an extreme, since we all demonstrate the tendencies of this type (as well as those of the other types) at least occasionally. The scatter diagram of behaviors in Exhibit 8-4 is a more accurate representation of most people who fit into the category of Socialite.

EXHIBIT 8-4

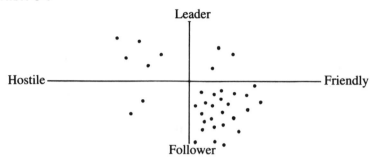

Bureaucrat

Bureaucrats (Exhibit 8-5) are people who always "go by the book" because "rules were made for good reasons." They rarely take chances and do not wish to stand out from the crowd. Neither do they desire to be leaders, although they resent those who are. Bureaucrats frequently gossip about people, but shy away from confronting them. Whenever a new idea is suggested, the Bureaucrat usually has a reason why it won't work and why it shouldn't even be tried. Of course, like the Socialite, the Bureaucrat is an extreme representation. These people have an "I'm *not* OK, you're *not* OK" orientation.

EXHIBIT 8-5
Hostile + Follower = Bureaucrat.

Leader

BUREAUCRAT	

Hostile   Friendly

Follower

Dictator

Dictators (Exhibit 8-6) are very dogmatic and always have to be right. Whenever they are wrong, they attempt to bully their way through, often as loudly as possible. Dictators insist on being in control and tend to be contemptuous of others. The Dictator's favorite three words are "I," "me," and "myself." These people have hostile and unresponsive natures that often cause them to be labeled as aggressive (often with negative connotations). In a word, the Dictator feels that "I'm OK, and you're *not* OK."

EXHIBIT 8-6
Hostile + Leader = Dictator.

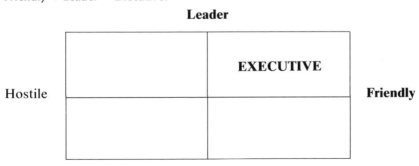

Executive

Executives (Exhibit 8-7) are independent thinkers who respect others' feelings and opinions, but make up their own minds about things. Natural leaders in any group, they are social, polite, and friendly, but not insincere in their emotions. When necessary, Executives are able to set limits on both themselves and others. The warmth of their dominant behavior often causes

EXHIBIT 8-7
Friendly + Leader = Executive.

Leader

	EXECUTIVE

Hostile **Friendly**

Follower

them to be viewed as admirably assertive rather than aggressive. The Executive's orientation is "I'm OK, you're OK."

In the chapters that follow, we will explore how you can expect prospects and clients to react to your presentations, based upon their psychological profile. Later in this section of the book, we will show you how to quickly build an effective relationship with any of these four types.

CHAPTER 9

The Socialite:
A Friendly Follower

These prospects or clients (Exhibit 9-1) initially appear to be ideal: They assume that the financial consultant has their interests at heart and give the impression of being easily maneuvered. Socialites are warm, friendly, quick to convince, and display a ready enthusiasm about any ideas you present. They are also very *talkative*.

EXHIBIT 9-1
Socialite Client.

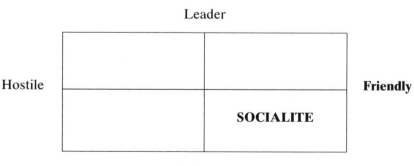

However, they also tend to have difficulty making decisions, and while they *appear* to be enthusiastic about a presentation, they will frequently end the conversation by saying that they need more time (usually to talk your ideas over with someone else). They tend to meander and socialize during the presentation and frequently have to be brought back to the subject at hand. Even when they do listen, they often miss part of the material. Some Socialites have strong dependency needs ("You're OK, I'm not OK"), and are looking for security. This is manifested in their desire to take the most popular path and keep primarily to "safe" investments. They don't wish to risk losing either their money or the opinion of others.

General Guidelines

When working with the Friendly Follower, you should remember this individual's need for acceptance and emphasize benefits that deal with acceptance, esteem, and security needs. Concentrate on products that are both safe and popular. Some of these investments are: certificates of deposit; popular, high-quality mutual funds; insurance; and investment-grade, well-known securities (be sure that investing in the market is in vogue before suggesting securities).

Remember that the Friendly follower needs to socialize. Meet this need, but do not allow it to override the purpose of the call. Firmly guide him through the presentation and be specific in your recommendations. Don't take the Socialite's enthusiasm and easy acceptance at face value. Probe for underlying doubts. Finally, rely primarily on closed probes (they will not encourage the meandering that an open probe might), and use summary and reflective statements frequently. This individual can be sold by accentuating how your product or service will meet his needs for safety and approval from friends and others.

EXAMPLE:

F.C.: Ms. Jones, insured certificates of deposit are one of our most *popular* investments among people who, like yourself, are interested in achieving a good rate of return with excellent *safety*. They're very pleased with them, and I'm sure that you will be as well.

Or:

F.C.: Mr. Smith, a mutual fund is the most *popular* method for accumulating wealth. Most *smart people* allow responsive, professional managers to do their work for them. I wouldn't be surprised to find that *many of your friends* own some of these funds. As various people talk about their investments, you can easily *participate* in the conversation because you'll own basically the same thing.

CHAPTER 10

The Bureaucrat:
A Hostile Follower

Hostile followers (Exhibit 10-1) tend to believe that FCs are only out to sell them something they neither need nor want. However, unlike their more aggressive counterparts, the Hostile Leaders, they deal with this through avoidance behavior such as silence and noncommittal responses. Bureaucrats do not make decisions well. Unlike the Socialites, they speak very little.

EXHIBIT 10-1
Bureaucrat Client.

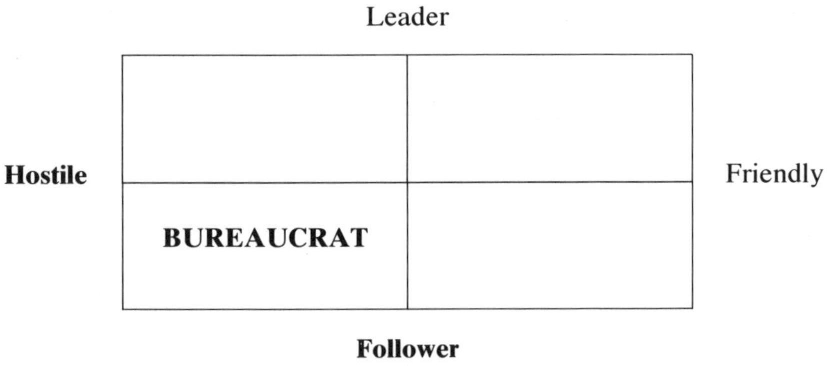

Leader

BUREAUCRAT	

Hostile   Friendly

Follower

Bureaucrats' poor self-image and deep lack of trust lead them to suspect that others are trying to take advantage of them ("I'm *not* OK, you're *not* OK"). Hence they require constant reassurance and support. As a result, they may appear to go along with a presentation but fail to make a decision. They do this by asking for more time and then making themselves inaccessible. While an aggressively hostile person will reject something out of hand, this more passive-aggressive individual will avoid confrontation but still fail to cooperate.

General Guidelines

Be conscious of the Bureaucrat's security needs and stress benefits that will meet them. Don't push. Go slowly and be patient. Take the time to communicate your genuine interest and establish the trust this individual seeks. It is important to guide firmly but gently. Draw out the Bureaucrat's feelings with open probes, pauses, and brief assertions of interest on your part. Remember, the Hostile follower requires safety and will prefer products with a "proven track record." This type of investment includes: certificates of deposit, investment-grade bonds, insurance, and, occasionally, investment-grade stocks and mutual funds.

Emphasize that what you are recommending is a traditional, accepted, prudent type of investment.

EXAMPLE:

FC: Ms. Jones, a municipal bond is one of the *most conservative* investments available to meet your need for tax-free income. It has *traditionally* been the *method of choice* selected to solve this kind of problem.

Or:

FC: Mr. Smith, a mutual fund is the most *traditional* and *judicious* method of accumulating wealth. It will allow you to *prudently* invest your money while achieving the added safety offered by diversification.

CHAPTER 11

The Dictator: A Hostile Leader

Dictators (Exhibit 11-1) are very difficult to work with because they have the preconceived idea that all FCs are corrupt and are only interested in making money, often at the client's expense. These prospects or clients tend to make flat assertions, to be sarcastic and argumentative, and to interrupt. They have strong security and esteem needs, which they maintain by trying to take control and rising above everyone else ("I'm OK, you're

EXHIBIT 11-1
Dictator Client.

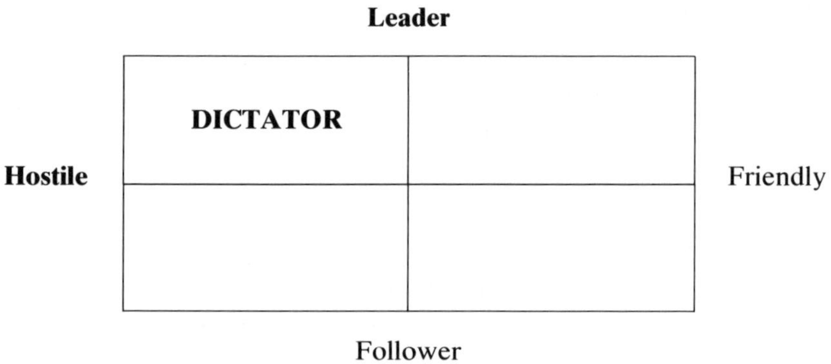

Leader

DICTATOR	

Hostile   Friendly

Follower

not OK''). Dictators are best handled through the use of assertive warmth (see the Executive FC traits in chapter 13 and the CLAPing skills covered in Chapter 7. The rapport-building skills discussed in Section Four are also very powerful in working with this type of client or prospect.)

One good thing about Dictators is that they can, and will, make decisions. Because of their need to appear better than others, these clients are often willing to take risks that others will shun. However, they can also become very hostile and quick to blame the FC if the risk does not pay off. Dictators like products that appeal to their ego needs.

General Guidelines

Whenever the Dictator resists or becomes hostile, communicate your desire to understand, your willingness to listen, and your ability to meet his needs. As you successfully communicate your sincere interest, the Dictator's behavior will frequently change from hostility and agressiveness to an assertiveness that is less defensive, if not actually warm. Remember that this individual has a strong *need* to trust, but fears that he will get "burned." How long it takes to win the Dictator's trust will vary according to the individual (and some will never trust an FC). However, once trust is won, the Hostile Leader will frequently become the most loyal and easiest-to-work-with client.

You can suggest such investments as: securities that are expected to turn a quick profit, high-performance mutual funds, insurance products that provide a large return on investment, and "sophisticated products."

Remember to stress the aspects of your product or service that will enhance the Dictator's self-esteem and independence. Also remember that the Hostile Leader needs to feel that he or she is different from, and therefore superior to, others.

EXAMPLE:

FC: Ms. Jones, we are only showing this investment opportunity to a *few* of our clients who we feel *have the experience* to really benefit from what it will provide.

Or:

FC: Mr. Smith, this mutual fund will allow you to *achieve the independence* you want. It will let you *do your own thing.* Because of the particular features of this fund, you can basically divorce yourself from the market and concentrate on what you want. You'll be *one of the very few* to recognize this opportunity—which means that you *stand apart from the crowd.*

When he is upset, let the Dictator express his feelings and then use CLAPping techniques to reassure him. Always be sure that you have dealt with his opinions and concerns before bringing up your own, or he will not hear you. Don't let him upset you—stick to your guns and refuse to be bullied. Frequently this individual really wants someone dependable to be in charge. If you buckle, he won't believe in your ability to help protect him from his own bad decisions. Make use of open probes, reflective statements, and summary statements (techniques covered in Section Two, "Communication Skills").

CHAPTER 12

The Executive:
A Friendly Leader

Executives (Exhibit 12-1) expect you to understand them, to meet their needs, and to effectively communicate to them how you will meet those needs. Executives are willing to listen and are open to new ideas, but will be impatient with "hype." Do everything possible to involve these clients in the decision-making process while using open probes to determine their needs.

EXHIBIT 12-1
Executive Client.

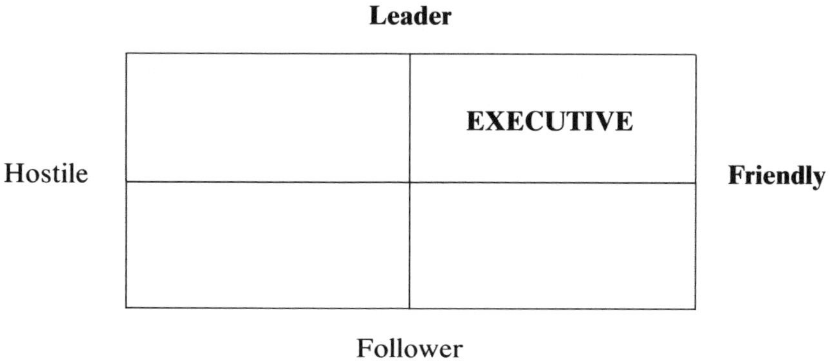

Leader

	EXECUTIVE

Hostile   **Friendly**

Follower

Be assertive and guide Executives through the presentation, but do not attempt to oversell or manipulate them. They will respond to respect and will return it, with loyalty. These Friendly Leaders are goal-oriented and capable of making decisions. They are emotionally secure and have a positive self-image that lets them be open to others ("I'm OK, you're OK"). They will respond to the steak as well as the sizzle.

General Guidelines

Always emphasize the end benefits of the Executive's decisions by showing how your product or service will help him to achieve his goals. Demonstrate how the features of the solution that you have selected correspond to the parameters of his problem. You can show an Executive any product or service as long as you tie its features into his needs.

Involve the Executive to the point that the decision that he makes is always an "informed decision." For example:

FC: Ms. Jones, this XYZ stock is both investment grade (*meeting your requirements for high quality*) and expected to grow at a rate of 12 percent per year over the next five years (*which exceeds your requirement of 8 percent growth*). What do you think?

Or:

FC: Mr. Smith, this mutual fund offers you the greatest probability of *meeting your goals of* A and B with C. Specifically, diversification and professional management will also allow you to *achieve the following benefits:* L, M, and N.

CHAPTER 13

Financial Consultant Personality Types

The same personality types that apply to clients also apply to financial consultants.

The Socialite FC

Socialite FCs (Exhibit 13-1) feel that clients are nice people who will buy from their friends. Hence they attempt to make

EXHIBIT 13-1
Socialite Financial Consultant: The Friendly Follower.

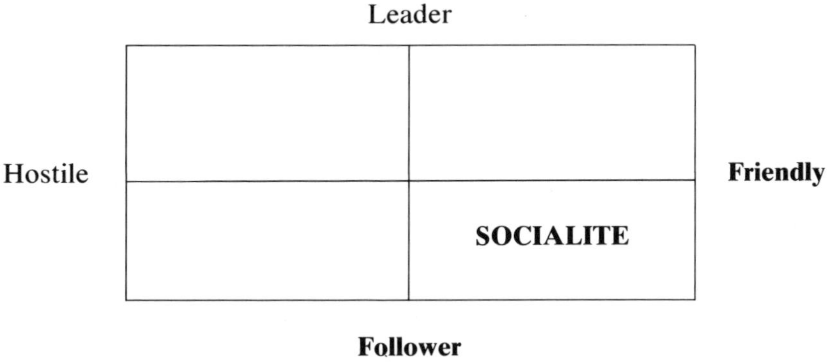

Leader

Hostile   Friendly

SOCIALITE

Follower

friends with all their prospects. They are warm, friendly, and well-liked around the office. However, because they dislike unpleasantness, they have a tendency to avoid making decisions or confronting clients (this can include reluctance to push closing a sale).

Socialite FCs are particularly vulnerable to rejection. As a result, they frequently don't like to cold-call. While they are very good at establishing rapport, they are often insufficiently assertive to maintain production.

The Bureaucrat FC

This kind of FC (Exhibit 13-2) is relatively rare. Bureaucrat FCs don't relate well to others and resent authority, yet

EXHIBIT 13-2
Bureaucrat Financial Consultant: The Hostile Follower.

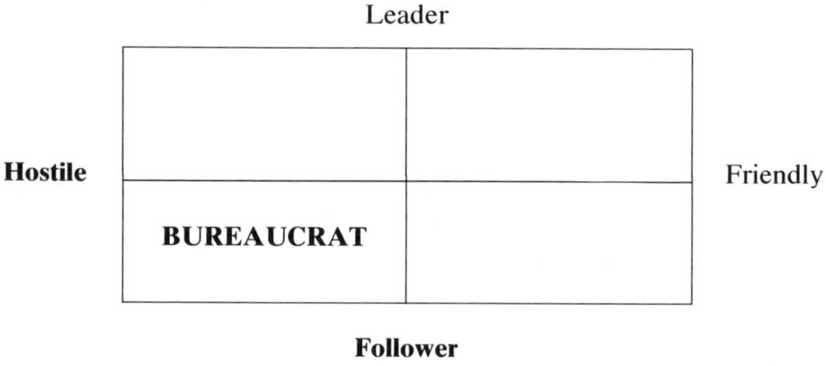

will rarely "buck" authority openly. They are passive-aggressive in their relationships, and their resentment is frequently transparent within a short time. For example, when a new product or sales campaign is inaugurated, the Bureaucrat has all the reasons why it won't work.

Bureaucrats feel that clients don't trust FCs and that customers will buy only when they are ready. They also believe that there is little they can do to influence customers to buy. Bureaucratic FCs are slow to make decisions, but will follow orders to the letter simply to avoid criticism. Often the closest they come to success is in following specific directions to make a specific number of calls per day and to read a specified script. They demonstrate little creativity or leadership and, in the end, are little more than order takers. Their behavior parallels that of the classic bureaucrat.

The Dictator FC

According to many clients, this is the most common type of FC. Dictator FCs (Exhibit 13-3) think of selling as a win-lose

EXHIBIT 13-3
Dictator Financial Consultant: The Hostile Leader.

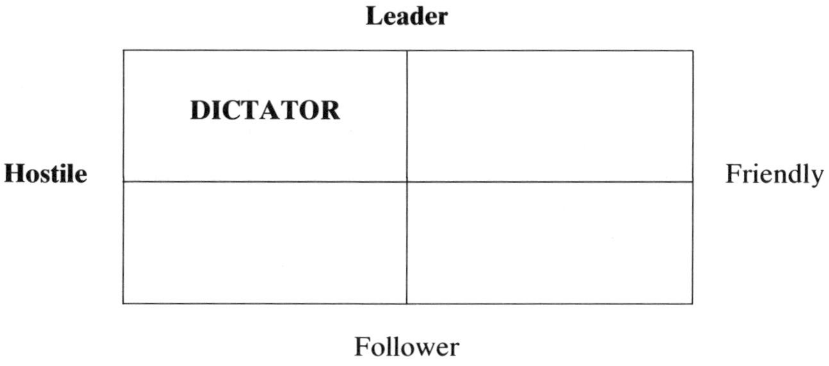

Leader

DICTATOR	

Hostile   Friendly

Follower

situation. As a result, they perceive the client as prepared to resist any sale and feel they must overwhelm that resistance. They communicate in an adversarial manner and tend to use force and manipulation to obtain a sale. Dictatorial FCs believe that the end justifies the means.

In the long run, their relationship style is at best self-defeating. While they may temporarily excel in production quotas, eventually they lose customers for the firm. Hostile Leaders are rarely trusted by their clients because their style does not establish rapport. A term frequently associated with them is "arrogant."

The Executive FC

The Executive (Exhibit 13-4) is the ideal FC and therefore will be explored at length later. Essentially, Executive FCs believe that clients will buy if they understand how the product or

EXHIBIT 13-4
Executive Financial Consultant: The Friendly Leader.

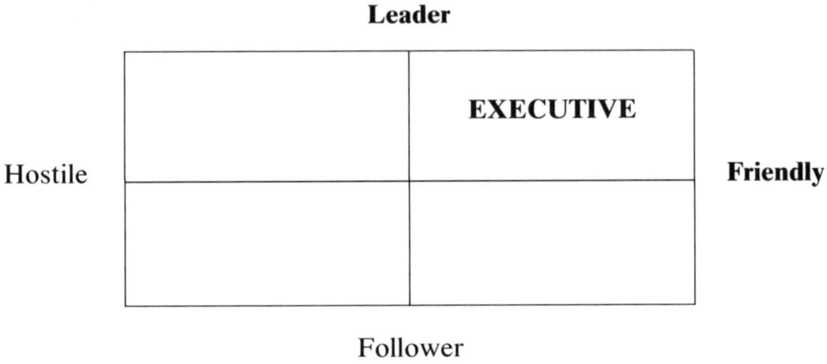

Leader

	EXECUTIVE

Hostile   **Friendly**

Follower

service being presented will meet their needs. They probe and profile their clients to determine and understand their needs. Then they link the appropriate features of the products or services to those needs so they can demonstrate the benefits to the client. Because we think the Executive FC demonstrates the traits of the ideal financial consultant, we've listed them below.

The Ideal Financial Consultant (The Executive FC)

The ideal FC manifests a series of qualities and attitudes in his work and the way he relates to others. While almost no one demonstrates all of these qualities all the time, the traits listed below have been found to be most effective and are worth having as goals.

Relationship to Self

The ideal FC is flexible, open, and growth-oriented. He is objective about himself, able to admit weaknesses and accept strengths, goal-oriented and self-motivating, creative, and able to make decisions and act on them. The good FC wants to use his talents to go as far as possible as fast as he can, but his ambition is tempered by concern and respect for others.

Relationship to Others

The ideal FC maintains good relationships with others and rarely appears as a threat to them. At the same time, he is assertive and forceful, capable of exercising dominance without appearing hostile. The ideal FC displays respect for other people's ideas and refuses to manipulate or exploit.

Relationship to Others in the Company

The model FC understands his role in the organization and the organization's importance to him. He relates to others reciprocally, by trying to develop effective and mutual working relationships. In addition, he gives all he's got and expects others to do the same. The ideal FC is a natural leader.

Attitude Toward Competition

This prototype takes competition in stride by doing his best to outwork and outsell his competitors. He studies competitive products and keeps abreast of competitive activity. He tends to arrive early and stay late at work.

Job Satisfaction

The ideal FC gets deep satisfaction from the job as long as he feels he is growing. His morale sags if he feels thwarted in his progress.

CHAPTER 14

Relationship Styles

We've already pointed out that no one is always a Dictator, a Bureaucrat, a Socialite, or even an Executive. Those who are Dictators at the office are often Socialites when playing with their children at home. This is an important point: Each of us demonstrates each of the personality types at different times, depending upon the context.

EXAMPLES:

- At work, the warm, decisive leadership of the Executive type is consistently the most appropriate.
- For a soldier in battle, the hostile aggressiveness of the Dictator is often most effective.
- When learning a new skill or job, the conservative, by-the-book mode of the Bureaucrat may work best.
- When relaxing and having fun with our family and friends, the carefree warmth of the Socialite often seems best.

The key to relating to others is flexibility. When we relate to everyone in the same way regardless of the context, we become locked into a rigid system that becomes self-defeating. In sales, we frequently run into clients or prospects who relate to us in a rigid style: They invariably exhibit the same personality type.

Have you ever had a client who always wanted you to make the decisions, but then found some reason for not going along with your ideas? Or one who always demanded that you do things his way, even when you knew he was wrong, and then blamed you when things went badly?

How did you respond to these clients? When the first client left all of the decisions up to you, did you make the decisions or try to involve him? When the second client tried to dominate you, did you give in or did you fight back? Whenever we get locked into a relationship that demands constant dominance on our side and constant submissiveness on the client's (or vice versa), we have developed a "relationship style" with that client that will be frustrating and self-defeating.

Relationship style describes the way two people commonly communicate within a given relationship. The manner in which an individual relates usually varies according to both the context and the person being related to. However, some people adopt a style of relating common to all contexts with a given person or even to all their relationships. When this happens, problems almost always occur.

We will describe three basic styles of relating: complementary, symmetrical, and parallel.

The Complementary Style

The complementary relationship is one of opposites; that is, dominant-submissive, introvert-extrovert, hostile-warm, healthy-sick, and so forth.

The most common form is dominant-submissive. This is a rigid mode in which one person is *always* in control, while the other is *never* in control. Conflicts are generally resolved when the submissive person withdraws in defeat or the dominant person hands down an edict. You can see this whenever a Dictator relates to a Bureaucrat or a Socialite.

EXAMPLES:

- The aggressive FC and the pliant, eager-to-please client.

- The domineering FC and the resistant prospect who is finally "won over," but who never sends back the necessary paperwork to open the account.

- The hostile client and the overaccommodating FC (who can't seem to make a sale).

- The hostile prospect and the FC who caves in rather than attempt to overcome resistance.

You should recognize that your submissive client receives a great "payoff" for playing the submissive role and will therefore try to maintain that role in your relationship. Don't let him. Move into the Executive mode and lead him to make his own decision, and then support it (even if it's not the decision you wanted). As you do so, he will begin to see you as a source of support instead of a threat and will learn to take more responsibility for his decisions.

Note that the submissive client retains an all-powerful veto—he may appear to "surrender," or go along with what you wish, but then fail to follow through with whatever has been "agreed upon." Thus you are placed in the position of having "won" temporarily without obtaining your final goal. Deal with "buyer's remorse" before it occurs! Remember, dominating your clients can, in the end, be very self-defeating.

The Symmetrical Style

The symmetrical style of relating is found in situations in which both individuals respond identically—for example, both are dominant or both are submissive. When both parties seek power or control, neither will give in, and the struggle escalates until serious difficulties arise. Neither person feels sufficiently sure of himself, the other person, or the relationship to relinquish control voluntarily. As a result, power becomes the primary source of validation in the relationship: "If I were really OK, I'd win."

When you run into an aggressive prospect or client, do you find yourself confronting him and trying to overpower him? Or when you work with a passive client, do you have difficulty closing the sale because you can't make yourself press for a commitment? In both situations, you and the client are responding identically to each other, and nothing is accomplished. In both cases, the client controls the outcome. All he needs to do to "win" is *nothing*. He can even just hang up.

Whenever you meet a Dictator, Bureaucrat, or Socialite client in that mode yourself, you risk a symmetrical interaction. Move into the Executive mode and show the Dictator that you are not threatened or defensive, but that you also do not need to threaten. Demonstrate your interest and confidence, and he will change his mode. When working with Bureaucrats or Socialites, use your Executive skills to support them and help them to make decisions. If neither of you takes the lead, nothing can be accomplished.

The Parallel Style

The parallel style is the healthiest and most effective of the three styles of relating because it is the most flexible. It's a style in which neither you nor your client feels anxious about the other, and you both feel able to express yourselves without fear that a struggle will develop. In addition, you both decide the issues of power and control by the needs of the situation rather than by arbitrary or conflicting expectations.

In practice, you, as the Executive in the relationship, are able to maintain the necessary flexibility by supporting your client's needs for self-esteem while providing the leadership to solve his problem. It is a relationship in which neither of you "wins" all the time. In addition, the rapport you build is based upon honesty, openness, trust, and cooperation.

In the sales relationship, the parallel style occurs when you and your client work together to solve his problems. In most cases, a parallel relationship will result in your taking the lead in seeking and proposing solutions to the client. However, the client accepts responsibility for the end decision in every case.

FLEXIBILITY IS AN IMPORTANT KEY TO COMMUNICATING.

Four elements are common to all three relationship styles: control, communication patterns, change, and decision making. It is the variations among and within these four elements that determine the style of interaction or relationship.

- *Control* consists of the way each person in a relationship attempts to manipulate or coerce the other in order to maintain control of a situation and/or the relationship itself. This element can be seen whenever you or your prospect/client attempts to manipulate the other to obtain your own ends. (*Note:* Attempts to manipulate are almost always construed as negative by the person being manipulated.)

- *Communication* consists of each person's willingness to participate in an exchange between peers rather than attempting to control the flow of information. How open is the flow of communication between you and your clients? Are you perceived as someone who communicates freely with your clients or who only calls when you have something to sell? Do you perceive your clients as clearly sharing data about their needs, goals, and concerns, or as only calling you when they have a complaint?

- *Change* consists of each person's willingness to risk change in his own behavior, as well as in the relationship itself, without feeling threatened. This element can be seen when you feel the need to suggest a change in strategy from one product line to another. How well does your client handle the change?

- *Decision making* consists of each individual's ability and willingness to place the needs of the relationship above his own desires relative to the decision at hand. At times, you may feel that a particular product or service is exactly what your client needs to solve a given problem but the client does not agree. Are you prepared to follow the client's preference rather than risk damaging the relationship by insisting on your own point of view? On the other side, is the client willing to trust your judgment?

The elements of control, communication, change, and decision making will vary from relationship to relationship. In a parallel relationship, each of you will take your turn at the appropriate time. The dominance, or overuse, of any element is usually less effective than a more or less equal mixing of these four factors.

BUILDING RAPPORT

Ask yourself, "Who is the most fascinating person in the world?" The answer will probably be, "I am! At least to me." And the second most fascinating person is an individual just like me. The more closely someone resembles us, the more comfortable we are with that person. We tend to listen to the person who thinks like us, who "speaks our language," and who sees things the same way we do (even if he doesn't agree with us).

Have you ever experienced an immediate feeling of ease with someone you've just met? Or have you had an encounter in which you and the other person intuitively "hit it off"? What about the opposite situation: Have you ever met someone in whose presence you feel immediately uncomfortable? The difference between the two kinds of encounters is that you experienced something called *rapport* in one and not in the other.

What is rapport? It might be defined as a comfortable feeling that you have when you are with some people you intuitively like. It is very much like empathy. Rapport helps us to communicate our understanding and acceptance of the other person. Yet the ability to develop rapport with someone else goes far beyond the words we use when we speak. In fact, some psychologists estimate that as much as 90 percent of communication occurs on an unconscious level and has little or nothing to do with what is being discussed. That is why it is possible to develop deep levels of rapport with someone with whom you disagree.

Have you noticed that some people seem to establish rapport naturally, while others have great difficulty? Why is one person very popular, successful, and listened to very carefully, while another, who may be much more intelligent, is ignored and has difficulty developing client relationships? One reason may be their level of interest in people. Another reason is that they may naturally be doing the things that allow rapport to occur.

We said earlier that the second most fascinating person in the world to most of us is someone who is very much like us. A close third is someone who communicates a genuine interest in us. Therefore, whenever you focus your attention on someone and genuinely try to understand what that person is saying, you almost automatically begin to build rapport. How to develop, enhance, and maintain rapport on the unconscious level is the subject of the next five chapters.

WE LIKE PEOPLE WHO LIKE US AND WHO ARE LIKE US.

Pacing

The key to the development of unconscious rapport is a process called *pacing*. We pace another person by being in physical, mental, and emotional alignment with him. Essentially, pacing is a way of becoming similar to another person.

Since we respond to people on three primary levels—physical, mental, and emotional—people we relate to on multiple levels often become our friends. Those to whom we don't relate never get close to us. One way to increase the chances of making someone a client, or a friend, is to become as much like that person as possible.

We have already shown that you unconsciously use many techniques in building rapport whenever you genuinely attend to someone. Conscious appreciation of what you already know how to do will enable you to consistently accomplish the same thing whenever you wish. It will also help you to deepen any rapport that you have already established.

Pacing blends a number of different methods, no one of which is sufficient to accomplish rapport by itself. *It is the combined effect of all the methods of pacing that will guarantee your ability to establish rapport with virtually anyone.* Although rapport has a number of aspects and each aspect is important, it is the cumulative effect that ultimately makes each aspect powerful.

CHAPTER 15

Mirroring the Client's Body Language

Have you ever been in a restaurant and, without over-hearing other people's conversations, been able to distinguish the friends and lovers from the antagonists among your fellow diners? How did you know? Unconsciously, we can tell who is in rapport and who is not. In this chapter, we begin to explore the rapport-building process.

As we said before, whenever we are very interested in people (or in what they have to say), we tend to psychologically open ourselves to their influence. In doing so, we also tend to follow their lead and to unconsciously seek deeper levels of rapport. Matching their body posture is one of the ways that we do this.

Matching Your Client's Body Posture—Mirroring

Remember, people like those who are most like them-selves—literally and figuratively. Matching body posture is one of the easiest and most effective ways of unconsciously influenc-ing your client.

Matching is just what is sounds like: copying, almost as a mirror image, your client's posture, breathing, and gestures. This doesn't mean that you have to be exact. Neither does it mean mimicking your client by moving as he moves (that would be noticeable and perhaps insulting). What it does mean is that anyone observing you and your client would soon notice many similarities in posture and gesture.

When you first meet someone, observe how he sits and then sit the same way. If you allow him to sit first, this is easy. If you are already seated, simply readjust your posture after he sits. Have you been at a party and noticed that three people sitting together on a couch almost always sit the same way? If one of them changes posture, they all change. That is matching on an unconscious level.

When your client adjusts his posture, wait a few moments and then *casually* adjust your own posture to match. As long as you wait, your shift will rarely be noticeable. Remember, we are social beings and it is natural for us to establish rapport. As you sit, stand, or gesture like your client, you unconsciously communicate to him a shared means of expression. This is true because our manner of sitting, standing, and gesturing is a very powerful means of communicating, and anyone who does these things as we do is communicating in the same way we are—and thus "speaking our language" at one level.

Matching may feel awkward at first. You may even feel the need to do so interferes with your presentation. (That is a natural feeling.) However, you already match very well at least part of the time, and you do so without thinking about it. With a little practice, you'll be able to match your client's body posture whenever you wish and still not have to think about it.

Test this notion for yourself. During a conversation with a friend or family member, begin to match the other person. Notice how the conversation progresses. Then, after a few minutes, change your posture to mismatch the other person as completely as possible, and notice what happens to the conversation. After just a few minutes, match the other person's body language again and note what happens to the conversation again. What differences did you notice in yourself and in the other person?

Initially, some people feel awkward following this proce-dure. However, with a little practice, it should become automatic. You will find that your interactions with people are more comfortable and easygoing as you employ these techniques.

As you are matching, you may notice the other person shifting his body posture so that you are no longer matched. Merely wait a few moments and then *casually* change your position until you are again somewhat matched. The key is to match as casually and subtly as possible.

Sometimes simple matching is not enough. Occasionally you will run into someone who is extremely fidgety. Trying to continuously match a person who can't seem to sit still would not only be difficult, but would also make you uncomfortable. A technique for dealing with this is called *cross matching*.

Cross Matching

When you are with a client who shifts his body position often, matching him move for move could make him aware that you are mimicking him. This could damage the very rapport that you are trying to establish. To avoid this and still continue to match, you can utilize a technique known as *cross matching:* Match some part of your body to a *different part* of your client's body.

EXAMPLE:
- If your client is sitting with legs crossed, cross your arms but keep your feet flat on the floor.
- If your client's arms are crossed, cross your wrists, legs, or ankles.
- A prospect who leans back in his chair might be cross matched by leaning to the side and slightly back.
- If the client puts his hand on his chin, put your hand near your head. As long as your hand is in a *similar* position, you're fine.
- If a prospective customer is sitting with his legs spread apart, leave your arms open.

The real key to matching is to adjust your body so that your posture *resembles* your client's posture.

Now, what about that fidgety client?

- If your client tends to slowly bounce or move his legs to some internal rhythm, tap your fingers at the same rate that he moves his legs. There is very little chance that he will become conscious of what you are doing, yet you will be matching his body language enough to maintain rapport.

- An alternative to tapping your fingers is making slight, almost unnoticeable, head movements (like nodding your head slightly to the client's leg rhythm). Again, there is very little possibility that the client will notice this minute movement. Yet *his unconscious will be aware,* and this awareness will correlate the rhythm of the two individual movements and maintain, or even deepen, your rapport.

Movements this subtle might be difficult for a third person to observe. However, as along as you do this, you will increase the rapport that you need to develop really effective communication.

How do you know whether you've achieved rapport by matching your body posture to the client's?

Testing for Rapport

You need to test to determine if you have established rapport. One test is a process called *leading.*

Once you have matched a person's body posture for several minutes, change your posture slightly and wait a short interval (typically between two and forty seconds) to see whether your client readjusts his body posture to match yours. That is, once you change, does he follow your lead by repositioning himself? If he does, then you have established rapport on the unconscious level. If he does not, go back to matching him for a while, and then test again.

(*Note:* It is important to realize that often thirty seconds will pass before the "matchee" follows your lead by changing his posture. Don't expect him to follow your lead immediately. Remember, it often takes several minutes of matching before you can successfully lead.)

While verifying rapport is very useful, leading has an-other important application. When you lead your client to move from one posture to another, his physiological change will often bring about a corresponding psychological change.

You can test this by being aware of your own internal, emotional changes as you conduct the following experiments:

Experiment 1:

A. Notice exactly how you are currently sitting or standing and the internal feelings that you associate with that body po-sition.

B. Now change your posture to one that is either more relaxed or less relaxed, and again notice your internal feelings.

C. Now, sit absolutely straight, and then allow yourself to sink into the chair. Once again, notice your internal feelings.

In which position could you most easily carry on a casual conversation? In which would it be the most difficult?

Do you associate specific emotions with certain body postures? If you do connect certain psychological states with corresponding physical states, then consider the ramifications of this thought: You can influence your mental and/or emotional state just by changing your posture!

YOU CAN CHANGE HOW YOU THINK AND FEEL JUST BY CHANGING YOUR BODY'S POSTURE!

Experiment 2:

A. Take a moment and stand as you usually do when you are proud of something you've accomplished. Be sure that some-one watching you would be able to tell how proud you are. Stand tall, throw your shoulders back and your chest out, and smile.

B. Notice how easy it is in this position to remember the many times when you have felt proud of something you've done.

Note how those feelings return and how proud you actually begin to feel. Take a moment and relive one of those accomplishments fully. Experience it as if it were fresh. (To see how this exercise might help you when making a presentation, see Section Eight, "Managing Stress in Today's Financial Marketplace.")

C. Now change your posture and let your shoulders slump. Slouch and allow your chest to sink. Lower your head and your gaze. Note how the intensity of the feeling changed. Now return to your original "proud" position again.

Psychologists call these positions, or postures, *anchors*. Anchors allow you to modify your internal state merely by changing your body posture.

Leading Your Client

You have just demonstrated to yourself that you can change the way that you think and feel simply by changing the way you sit, stand, or breathe. Wouldn't it be useful to be able to move your client the same way? Now you can.

When you are speaking to a client who is in a "negative" state (i.e., any state that would keep him from listening openly and positively to what you are saying), you can *lead* him into a more positive state by following these two simple steps:

1. Establish rapport by matching your body to his.
2. Gradually shift your body into a posture that will lead him into a different mental state as his own associations take effect.

Remember that the client may have associations that are different from yours. So if the first state you lead him to is not an improvement, continue to lead him through different postures until you obtain the response you desire. Here are some examples:

• You may wish to lead an anxious client from a stiff or rigid posture/state to a relaxed posture/state.

- Try leading a customer who is very relaxed into a posture/state normally associated with paying close attention (e.g., sitting up straight, leaning slightly forward, maintaining good eye contact).
- Lead an irritable customer into a relaxed posture/state.
- Lead an indecisive client into a dynamic, decisive posture/state (e.g., such as the "proud" pose you experienced early).

As you combine leading a client's posture with leading his breathing and rate of speech, you will be able to achieve deeper levels of rapport and greater influence.

YOU CAN MODIFY YOUR CLIENT'S FEELINGS AND THINKING BY LEADING HIM INTO A MORE POSITIVE STATE!

Matching Breathing

Matching your rate of breathing to that of your client is one of the most powerful techniques for enhancing rapport. This is a simple technique whose impact occurs below the level of conscious awareness and, if combined with the previous techniques, can significantly increase your rapport level. To match breathing, simply breathe at the same rate as your client.

- If you are conversing, time your breathing to match the inhalations and exhalations of your client's speech rate. In addition, time your sentences to match his breathing. This can be especially effective when speaking on the telephone, since it is one of the few things you can match over the phone.
- Watch the rise and fall of your client's chest or shoulders, since this correlates with his breathing.
- There will be times when you do *not* wish to match a client's breathing (e.g., if the client suffers from asthma or emphy-

sema). At these times, use a cross-matching technique such as moving your head, finger, or foot at the same pace as the client's breathing.

As we mentioned before, matching your client's breathing and posture can significantly enhance the depth of your rapport. When you combine matching with the other rapport-enhancing techniques that we will discuss in upcoming chapters, you can become even more effective.

CHAPTER 16

Matching the Client's Speech

The "fast-talking salesman" and the "slow-minded customer" have become clichés. Yet, have you ever spoken with a person who talked so quickly that you felt rushed? How about one who spoke so slowly that you wanted to speed them up? Did you feel comfortable or uncomfortable as you conversed with such a person? Most of us feel at least some discomfort when confronted with an individual who is speaking too quickly or too slowly. Even when we can't quite put our finger on the problem, we know something is wrong.

If you felt uncomfortable when your client was too fast or too slow for you, remember the client probably felt the same way. If he was too slow for you, you were probably too fast for him. And vice versa. In such a case, both of you are slightly uncomfortable. Even though you may not be consciously aware of it, such differences contribute to what we call "bad vibes."

> **PEOPLE GENERALLY PREFER TO LISTEN AT THE SAME RATE AS THEY SPEAK.**

The traditional "hustler" salesman is always portrayed as a fast talker. It could be that he's just so excited about what he's selling that he gets carried away. Or he may be afraid that if he doesn't get his message across quickly, his customer will hang up before he reaches the close. Or perhaps he's just nervous. In any case, his rapid speech pattern can be self-defeating unless his customer speaks just as quickly.

Think about the last time you were a customer and the salesperson spoke so rapidly that you became uncomfortable. You may have needed time to think about all this fast-paced information, but to give you that time to think, the salesperson would have had to slow down. After all, it's not easy to listen to a fast talker *and* process what that person is saying at the same time. If the salesperson didn't slow down, one of three things probably happened:

1. You processed the information that you caught but you probably didn't hear everything the salesperson said.
2. You listened to everything the salesperson said, but you didn't get a chance to think about any of it.
3. You tried to both listen and process and ended up confused.

It should be obvious that frustration is an almost inevitable result of any of these possibilities. After all, asking clients to absorb information and make a decision without thinking about it shows little respect for them and frequently makes them feel "pushed." At the same time, speaking too slowly can leave clients bored and just as frustrated. Hence:

**MATCHING THE CLIENT'S SPEECH
CAN HELP YOU BUILD RAPPORT!**

Remember, in order to think, you need time. If you get the time you need, you can make a decision and act upon it. If you don't, you are likely to feel pressured and frustrated or confused. Show your client the same thoughtful respect that you would like shown to you.

Of course, some people who don't speak quickly are very fast thinkers, nonetheless. How can you tell when your client is following you? Note his expression, the relevance of his questions, and changes in his voice quality, speed, tone, or affect that might be indicators. As a general rule, though, if you speak more slowly than your customer, speed up. If you speak faster, slow down.

Leading

In the last chapter, we showed how you could test for rapport through physical leading. (Once you think you have established rapport, simply modify your posture slightly and see if the client follows your lead. If he does, you know you have established rapport.) You can also test for rapport by modifying your speech.

Once you have matched a client's rate of speech, you can incrementally change your own rate, making it either faster or slower, and see if the client follows your lead. If he does, you know you have established rapport. A client will usually follow you without even consciously becoming aware that he is doing so. Verbal leading might help you:

- Increase the effectiveness of any sales presentation. For example, suppose that in a previous conversation, your client had spoken enthusiastically, *and quickly,* when referring to a great business triumph (or a hobby or something else that interested him). You realize that, for him, speaking quickly is correlated with enthusiasm. Having mentally noted this, you might incrementally increase the speed of your presentation until both *you* and your client are speaking at his "enthusiasm" rate. While this won't guarantee the sale, it will significantly increase your chances.
- Build additional rapport during a prospecting interview.
- Make a proposal to your boss.
- Calm down an upset client (initially match his rate of speech, and then lead him into a calmer state by gradually slowing your own rate of speech).

Verbal and physical leading techniques, when used with CLAPing, allow you to gather valuable information about the client. Just imagine what you could accomplish if you really spoke the client's language. This is the subject of the next chapter.

CHAPTER 17

Matching the Client's Thinking Process

We have mentioned the concept of "speaking the client's language" several times. So far, we've shown how everything that you do (how you sit, stand, breathe, and speak) affects your ability to be like your client. Now let's look at language itself and the ways the words people use tell us something about how they think.

Have you ever heard a client say, "It *looks* good to me" or "It *sounds* good to me" or "It *feels* good to me"? These phrases, and others like them, provide important information about how people think or process information. By learning to recognize and use the clues your clients give you about how they think, you can literally communicate in a way that will make them perceive you as being just like them. This is a powerful tool since clients naturally "resist" people they perceive as "outsiders."

Some of us think by **seeing** images in our mind, others by discussing a concept with ourselves so as to **hear** how it sounds, while still others need to determine how something **feels.** Regardless of how we process information, we tend to verbalize our thoughts using words and phrases that most closely match how we think.

This is true for several reasons. Although we are born with five senses, we begin to rely upon one or two more than the others as we mature. This leads us to remember that aspect of an experience more completely than the others. Thus, if we rely upon sight, we are more likely to remember the visual aspects of an experience. As a result, when we relate an experience to someone, we will use visual terms to describe it. The same is true of each sense. For example:

- "I think that my favorite memory of spring is the *beautiful colors* that *appear* as the trees and flowers come into bloom. You can *see* spring everywhere. Even as you *watch* the birds return for the summer, their *colors* are enhanced as they prepare to mate." [**Visual**]
- "I think that my favorite memory of spring is the *sound* of children playing in the parks after a *silent* winter. You can *hear* spring everywhere, even as you *listen* for the first *song* of the robin building its nest and the *buzz* of the bumblebee moving from flower to flower." [**Auditory**]
- "I think that my favorite memory of spring is the first *sensation* of *warmth* from the spring sun after a *cold* winter. You can *smell* the flowers and the trees and *feel* the rebirth of the world around you." [**Kinesthetic**]

Of course, some experiences so forcefully impress themselves on a specific sense that we will remember them through that sense no matter which sense we habitually rely upon. For example, a cold shower would impress the kinesthetic sense, while a symphony would compel the auditory, and a rainbow the visual. Therefore, a person who relies primarily upon sight will still sometimes use auditory and kinesthetic terms.

Still, once we learn to rely upon one sense over the others, the data received through that sense dominate our thought processes. As a result, we may "specialize" in that sensory mode when we think. This means that if you think by making pictures, you probably habitually rely upon your sight and are therefore most aware of the visual aspects of your experiences. This doesn't mean that you aren't able to remember the sounds and feelings associated with an experience, but rather that they are not as "obvious" as what you see. If we use our other senses very infrequently, we can become confused when we receive too much information through them. Psychologists refer to this as *sensory overload.*

Since people understand the familiar more quickly than the unfamiliar, they comprehend words and phrases that most closely correspond to those they use in their own thinking process. In short, something as simple as our choice of words can make the difference between whether or not we are understood by others. For example, if your client uses words and phrases that are primarily visual (sight-oriented), and you use phrases that are primarily auditory (sound-oriented), you may well confuse the client.

You will be most successful if you use sensory-oriented words that match the way your client processes information. Try it and you'll be amazed at the improvement in understanding that occurs compared to the difficulty created when your words mismatch your client's particular sensory orientation.

Read the following scripts, and after you finish them, determine which financial consultant you think has the best chance of continuing the conversation.

Reading I

> *FC #1:* I just came across a report on a stock, the XYZ Company, that looks interesting, and if you have a moment, I'd like to show it to you.
>
> *Client:* Sounds interesting. I'd like to hear some more.
>
> *FC #1:* Well, I just saw something that shows that their earnings have really improved in the last few months.
>
> *Client:* What do you mean? I've heard that XYZ is in really bad shape.
>
> *FC #1:* Yet this financial report clearly shows that it has really improved, which is why you—
>
> *Client:* [*Interrrupting*] My gut reaction is that the company hasn't changed at all.
>
> *FC #1:* What have you seen to make you think that way? I perceive the change as very positive.

Client: Well, I've been hearing just the opposite.

FC #1: Look, I want to show you a few things that should give you a better picture.

What was your gut feeling as you read this dialogue? Were you comfortable, or did you feel the FC and the client weren't on the same wavelength? Go back and read it again, then go on to Reading II.

Reading II

FC #2: I just came across a report on a stock, the XYZ Company, that looks interesting, and if you have a moment, I'd like to show it to you.

Client: Sounds interesting. I'd like to hear some more.

FC #2: Well, I just heard something that states that their earnings have really improved in the last few months.

Client: What do you mean? I've heard that XYZ is in really bad shape.

FC #2: Yet this financial report clearly states that it has really improved, which is why you—

Client: [Interrupting] My gut reaction is that the company hasn't changed at all.

FC #2: What have you heard to make you think that way? I feel the change is very positive.

Client: Well, I've been hearing just the opposite.

FC #2: Listen, I want to tell you a few things that should give you a better feeling.

Which financial consultant do you think has the better chance to continue the conversation? Most people (and thousands have been tested) think that FC #2 has the better chance. They usually comment that FC #1 was more confrontational and aggressive. FC #2 is usually judged more supportive, understanding, and responsive.

Let's compare the two FCs word for word.

FC #1: I just came across a report on a stock, the

FC #2: I just came across a report on a stock, the

FC #1: XYZ Company, that looks interesting, and if

FC #2: XYZ Company, that looks interesting, and if

FC #1: you have a moment, I'd like to show it to you.

FC #2: you have a moment, I'd like to show it to you.

Client: Sounds interesting. I'd like to **hear** some more.

FC #1: Well, I just *saw* something that *shows* that

FC #2: Well, I just *heard* something that *states* that

FC #1: their earnings have really improved in the last few months.

FC #2: their earnings have really improved in the last few months.

Client: What do you mean? I've **heard** that XYZ is in really ***bad shape***.

FC #1: Yet this financial report clearly *shows* that

FC #2: Yet this financial report clearly *states* that

FC #1: it has really improved, which is why you—

FC #2: it has really improved, which is why you—

Client: [*Interrupting*] My **gut reaction** is that the company hasn't changed at all.

FC #1: What have you *seen* to make you *think* that way?

FC #2: What have you *heard* to make you *think* that way?

FC #1: I *perceive* the change as very positive.

FC #2: I *feel* the change is very positive.

Client: Well, I've been **hearing** just the opposite.

FC #1: Look, I want to *show* you a few things that

FC #2: Listen, I want to *tell* you a few things that

FC #1: should give you a better *picture*.

FC #2: should give you a better *feeling*.

If you're like most people, you're amazed that a few sensory words (mismatched to the client by FC #1 and matched to the client by FC #2) make all the difference. The change in response occurs outside of conscious awareness. Matching sensory words allows more effective communication and is a very worthwhile technique.

> **MATCHING THE CLIENT'S SENSORY STYLE CREATES MORE EFFECTIVE COMMUNICATION.**

EXAMPLE: Someone approaches you to discuss a new mutual fund and says, "I've been *looking over* this new mutual fund and I'm sure that you'll agree that it *shows* excellent potential. Let's take a minute and I'll put you in the *picture*." You might respond in any one of several ways:

A. It certainly *looks* good to me. Have you *shown* it to the other people in the office yet?"

B. "It certainly *sounds* good to me. Have you *told* the other people in the office about it yet?"

C. "It certainly *feels* good to me. Have you shared your *sense* of it with the other people in the office yet?"

All three responses *mean* essentially the same thing, don't they? But note the differences in word choice. Which response most closely matches the presenter's language? The first response. The other two mismatch the presenter's language and may actually result in a misunderstanding or confusion. The second and third responses might leave the presenter with the impression that you just can't *see* what he's getting at.

If you've ever tried to learn a foreign language, you probably recall having to mentally translate into English whatever was said by someone in that other language. When a client speaks to us in a sensory style different from our own (e.g., if we're speaking in visual terms and the other person replies in auditory or kinesthetic terms), we have to unconsciously translate what the client is saying into our terms. This takes a moment and can lead to confusion because the client is not "speaking our language.'' At this point, we can either shift gears and speak in the client's terms, or we can allow ourselves to become frustrated and annoyed. Which route we choose will depend upon how important it is to us to make the client comfortable.

Matching your clients' sensory-oriented words significantly enhances the communication process, while mismatching their words often increases the barriers that may exist between you. If you always seek to match your client's speaking style, you will find that figuratively, as well as literally, you will be able to speak their language.

Now you know how important it is to match a prospect's sensory orientation. But how do you open a conversation before you know what that orientation is? Just as there are words that match a particular sensory orientation, there are others that are neutral and can be used with any orientation. We call these words *unspecified,* and they can be very useful when opening a conversation with someone you don't know. For example: ''Ms. Jones, my company *anticipates* a rise in interest rates over the next quarter. As you *contemplate* this, would you be willing to *consider* a course of action that we are *advising* for our best clients?''

For your convenience, we have provided lists of sensory-oriented words and phrases in Exhibits 17-1 and 17-2.

Being able to ''speak the other person's language'' by matching his sensory words is valuable in virtually every situation in which it is important for us to relate to another. Do you know someone who has previously been difficult to communicate with?

Someone who doesn't *see* what you're *showing* him.

Someone who doesn't *hear* what you're saying.

Someone who doesn't *grasp* your *meaning*.

Try matching that person's sensory orientation in the language you use and see what a difference it makes—not only in your immediate communication, but also in your total relationship.

WE LIKE THOSE WHO ARE MOST LIKE OURSELVES.

EXHIBIT 17-1
Sensory-Oriented Words

Visual	Auditory	Kinesthetic	Unspecified
See	Sound	Feel	Think
Picture	Hear	Grasp	Decide
Appear	Mention	Firm	Motivate
Outlook	Inquire	Pressure	Understand
Imagine	Scream	Grip	Plan
Focus	Tune	Move	Know
Perception	Shrill	Flow	Consider
Foresee	Oral	Stress	Advise
Vista	Earful	Callous	Deliberate
Looks	Listen	Hard	Develop
Clear	Ring	Warm	Create
Observe	Resonate	Numb	Manage
Horizon	Loud	Dull	Repeat
Scope	Vocal	Hold	Anticipate
Notice	Remark	Affected	Indicate
Show	Discuss	Emotional	Admonish
Scene	Articulate	Solid	Activate
Watch	Say	Soft	Prepare
Aim	Announce	Active	Allow
Angle	Audible	Bearable	Permit
Aspect	Boisterous	Charge	Direct
Clarity	Communicate	Concrete	Discover
Cognizant	Converse	Foundation	Ponder
Conspicuous	Dissonant	Hanging	Determine
Examine	Divulge	Hassle	Resolve
Glance	Earshot	Heated	Meditate
Hindsight	Enunciate	Hunch	Believe
Illusion	Interview	Hustle	Cogitate
Illustrate	Noise	Intuition	Judge
Image	Proclaim	Lukewarm	Evaluate
Inspect	Pronounce	Motion	Reckon
Obscure	Report	Muddled	Imagine
Obvious	Roar	Panicky	Contemplate
Perspective	Rumor	Rush	Assume
Pinpoint	Screech	Sensitive	Conceptualize
Scrutinize	Silence	Set	Conceive
Sight	Speak	Shallow	Influence
Sketchy	Speechless	Shift	Accept

EXHIBIT 17-1
Continued

Visual	Auditory	Kinesthetic	Unspecified
Survey	Squeal	Softly	Prove
Vague	State	Stir	Depend
View	Tell	Structured	Communicate
Vision	Tone	Support	Comprehend

EXHIBIT 17-2
Sensory-Oriented Phrases

Visual	Auditory	Kinesthetic
An eyeful	Clear as a bell	All washed up
Appears to be	Clearly expressed	Boils down to
Bird's-eye view	Call on	Chip off the old block
Catch a glimpse of	Describe in detail	Come to grips with
Clear-cut view	Express yourself	Calm, cool and collected
Dim view	Give an account of	Firm foundation
Eye to eye	Give me your ear	Floating in thin air
Flashed on	Heard voices	Get a handle on
Get a perspective on	Hidden message	Get a load of this
Hazy idea	Hold your tongue	Get the drift of
In light of	Idle talk	Get your goat
In person	Idle tongue	Hand-in-hand
In view of	Inquire into	Hang in there
Looks like	Keynote speaker	Heated argument
Make a scene	Loud and clear	Hold it
Mental image/picture	Power of speech	Hold on
Mind's eye	Purrs like a kitten	Keep your shirt on
Naked eye	Outspoken	Lay cards on the table
Paint a picture	Rap session	Moment of panic
Photographic memory	Rings a bell	Not following you
Plainly see	State your purpose	Pull some strings
Pretty as a picture	To tell the truth	Sharp as a tack
See to it	Tongue-tied	Slipped my mind
Showing off	Tune in	Smooth operator
Sight for sore eyes	Tune out	Start from scratch
Staring off into space	Unheard of	Stiff upper lip
Take a peek	Voice an opinion	Stuffed shirt
Tunnel vision	Within hearing range	Topsy-turvy
Up front	Word for word	On the same track

CHAPTER 18

Think and Speak Positively

How many times has someone told you "Don't worry"? What did you do? You worried! "After all," you thought, "what am I supposed to *not* worry about?" The problem is that in order not to do something, we have to think about doing it first, and then consciously *not* think about it. Try this: *Don't think about the Statue of Liberty!* How did it work? If you're like most of us, you thought about the Statue of Liberty, even if only for a microsecond, before moving on to something else.

Interesting, isn't it? When you're on a diet, what are you supposed to *not* think about? Food, right? But what fills almost every waking thought? Food! The harder we try to push the thought of food out of our heads, the more attention we must focus on the thought (food) to do it. No wonder so many of us have difficulty losing weight. Our language mediates the way we think, and that is why in order to *not* think of something, we *have to* think about it first. Remember, we communicate with ourselves, and communication is the purpose of language.

What do you do when you lose something? You look for it until you find it. For many of us, the same thing happens when we *lose* weight. We seem to search until we have not only found every pound that we've lost, but a few more that we weren't even looking for.

DON'T THINK OR SPEAK NEGATIVELY!
Or, in better words:
THINK AND SPEAK POSITIVELY!

Considering the previous comments, have you thought about the effect of negative statements upon clients?

"Don't worry about the dividend."

The client has to think about potential dividend problems in order to *not* worry about them. The probability that the client will become concerned about dividend problems is then increased. After all, why would you bring the subject up if you didn't think there are potential problems with the dividend?

Here are some examples of negative statements that financial consultants are prone to make:

"Don't make a decision until you've heard what our research department has to say about the stock."
"Don't buy certificates of deposit at a bank."
"Don't forget."

These kinds of statements account for a lot of the misunderstandings and surprises that occur with clients. A client who forgets something important or brings up concerns about future dividends is only doing exactly what we unconsciously directed him to do. By our negative statements, we set ourselves up to obtain the very results that we wished to avoid.

We get a different, more desirable reaction from clients when we speak in positive terms. Transform the above negative statements into positive ones:

"You can depend upon the dividend."

"Look over what our analysts have to say before you make a decision on the stock."

"Look at all your alternatives carefully. We're confident you'll purchase your CD from us."

"Remember."

Words are very powerful because they direct the thoughts and memories of the listener. These thoughts and memories then influence the listener's attitudes, behaviors, and beliefs. If we accept

- that our unconscious mind cannot deal in negatives (try to think of nothing),

or

- that our minds have to focus briefly upon the unwanted concept in order to make sense of a negative statement,

then we get the following communications formula: **The Original Statement (OS) minus the Negation (N) equals the Unconscious Message Received (UMR).**

$$OS - N = UMR.$$

This means that a negative statement becomes unconsciously transformed into literally the opposite of what we intended, whether we are thinking to ourselves or talking to someone else. For example:

"Do not feel bad." − *not* = "Do feel bad."

"Do not forget." − *not* = "Do forget."

"I do not want to be late." − *not* = "I do want to be late."

"Do not worry about the next delivery." − *not* = "Do worry about the next delivery."

It's obvious how negative words can program us to fail in obtaining our objectives. Speaking in positives is much more effective. Remember:

SPEAK POSITIVELY!

CHAPTER 19

Discovering the Client's Buying Motivations

Psychologists have found that each of us has various criteria that we use to make decisions. Certain of these criteria may consistently dominate our decision making, the degree of dominance depending on the class of decision that we face (e.g., purchasing clothing versus choosing a friend).

Identifying the client's basic decision criteria, or motivational themes, is one of the concepts underlying "benefit selling." Instead of expecting your client to translate the features of your products or services into terms that are personally meaningful to him, you can facilitate the process by using his criteria to describe your products. This way, you speak his language and, once again, demonstrate that you think as he does. This concept will greatly assist you in closing a sale.

Try this exercise. Exhibit 19-1 lists common buying motivations (examples of equivalencies are given in Exhibit 19-3 at the end of this chapter). Identify as many reasons as possible for why a person might go to a particular gas station or clothing store. If you think of reasons or motivations that are not on the list, add them.

EXHIBIT 19-1
Buying Motivations

Alternatives available	Extras	Peer pressure
Appearance	Fear	Prestige
Brand name	Greed	Price
Cleanliness	Habit	Profit
Confidence	Identification	Quality
Convenience	Image	Relationship
Courtesy	Impulse	Safety
Credit	Integrity	Service
Curiosity	Money	Status
Dependability	Need	Suitability
Entertainment	Performance	Times open

On a separate piece of paper, or in the boxes below, list three to five words from your expanded list that identify your most important reasons for making the following decisions.

• Reasons you buy gas at a particular station.

```

```

• Reasons you go to a certain clothing store and buy certain clothing.

```

```

• Reasons for choosing a particular restaurant.

+---+
| |
| |
| |
| |
| |
+---+

• Reasons for choosing your current apartment or house, or one that you would like to buy.

+---+
| |
| |
| |
| |
| |
+---+

• Qualities you like in a friend (other than Need, Services, or Convenience).

+---+
| |
| |
| |
| |
| |
+---+

Once you have up to five words associated with each decision, search for words (equivalent or substantially equivalent; e.g., reputation = reliability = dependability) that appear in two decision areas. Copy these words into a separate group, or place them in the box on page 125.

Now underline all the words in the separate group that were used in three decision areas. Next, put an asterisk (*) next to the words that were used in four areas. Finally, put a double asterisk (**) next to the words used in all five areas. For example, one individual had the criteria listed in Exhibit 19-2.

EXHIBIT 19-2

Buying Motivations	Gas	Clothing	House	Friends	Restaurants
Appearance		X			
Atmosphere					X
Attractiveness				X	
Cleanliness	X				
Common interests				X	
Condition			X		
Credit	X				
Location	X				
Neighborhood			X		
Popularity		X		X	X
Price	X	X	X		X
Proximity				X	
Quality					X
Selection		X			X
Services	X				
Size			X		
Style		X	X		
Warmth				X	

A summary of this individual's criteria is provided in the box below.

> Price*
> Location/Neighborhood/Proximity
> Selection/Services/Interests in common*
> Appearance/Attractiveness/Cleanliness
> Style
> Popularity

This individual had six criteria that he used in making two or more decisions, five criteria that he used in making three or more decisions, and two criteria that he used in making four out of five decisions. When selling to this individual, it would be useful to stress price and selection, then popularity, convenience of location, and attractiveness. The chances are that he will probably buy what you are selling.

While not everyone has the same criteria, we have run this exercise with thousands of participants and found very similar results: That is, we all have criteria that affect multiple decisions. The lesson is obvious: Learn your clients' basic criteria so you can stress the applicable benefits of the products you are selling.

> **WE ALL HAVE CRITERIA THAT AFFECT MULTIPLE DECISIONS.**

If you know your clients' criteria, you will be able to make much more effective sales presentations. Instead of presenting a variety of features, benefits, and advantages and "hoping" that a client will "correctly translate" them into items that are personally meaningful, you can elicit your client's buying motivations and then tailor a presentation that is both directed and highly meaningful to your client. By combining an understanding of your client's

- emotional needs (see Chapter 8–12),
- sensory style of thinking and speaking (visual, auditory, or kinesthetic; see Chapter 17),

• buying motivations,

you can create a presentation that is formed entirely from his point of view and in his language. Such a presentation is almost impossible to resist.

EXAMPLE: Here is a presentation directed at a Socialite client who is primarily "visual" in orientation and whose criteria are the same as those provided in the example above (i.e., proximity/location; services/selection). The key words are italicized.

> *FC:* Ms. Jones, I'm sure that when you *look at* the insurance plan that I am going to *show* you, you will *see* why I think that it is so *attractive.* To begin with, it has many features that were *designed* to fit *beautifully* with the needs of a new business. That's why it is so *popular.* You can choose from a *selection* of several mutual funds, and you can change among the funds up to four times a year without charge. In addition, you'll receive a market letter each quarter to keep you up-to-date on the performance of each fund. This is just one of the *many services* offered by our firm. I think that you'll also like the convenience of our *location,* which will easily enable us to meet personally to review your needs. I'm sure that you'll find our service both warm and *friendly. Many* of your *neighbors* buy their insurance from us. Finally, we've been in business for over 150 years, which should give you a real sense of *security.*

Discovering your client's major buying motivations can be as simple as asking a few questions and listening carefully to the answers. This can be done easily over one or more casual conversations or during the "get acquainted" portion of a face-to-face meeting.

Simply ask your client questions that might normally come up in a social or business situation, such as what he likes about a given product or restaurant, and note the criteria that appear consistently in his answers. Read the dialogue below, looking for decision-making criteria enunciated by the client. We have italicized the important probes of the financial consultant.

> *FC:* Bill, I notice that you own a Jaguar. I'm thinking of buying one myself, but I haven't quite made up my mind. *What do you like about yours?*

Client: Well, I think it's a well-made car, and it's lots of fun to drive.

FC: Anything else?

Client: Yes. It's a sharp-looking car. Not like some of these boxes they're selling today. And my family likes it.

FC: Sounds great, Bill. But where do you get it serviced? I mean, I'd guess you'd want a factory-trained mechanic for it.

Client: That's for sure. I don't want to take any risks where a $60,000 car is concerned. I take it to a dealer two towns away.

FC: That's a little out of your way, isn't it? *What made you choose that dealer?*

Client: Frankly, Dick, I didn't like the quality of the service that I was getting at the dealer here in town, where I bought the car. The dealer I bring it to now always has the car when he says he will, and he does a quality job. For that, I don't mind the inconvenience of paying a little more and having the extra drive. Besides, he always gives me a loaner while the car's in the shop.

Did you notice all the information that the client provided? Let's go through the dialogue again, this time with the client's possible decision-making criteria italicized.

FC: Bill, I notice that you own a Jaguar. I'm thinking of buying one myself, but I hasn't quite made up my mind. What do you like about yours?

Client: Well, I think that it's a *well-made* car, and it's lots of *fun* to drive.

FC: Anything else?

Client: Yes. It's a *sharp-looking* car. Not like some of these boxes they're selling today. And my *family likes it.*

FC: Sounds great, Bill. But where do you get it serviced? I mean, I'd guess you'd want a factory-trained mechanic for it.

Client: That's for sure. I *don't want to take any risks* where a $60,000 car is concerned. I take it to a dealer two towns away.

FC: That's a little out of your way, isn't it? What made you choose that dealer?

Client: Frankly, Dick, I didn't like the *quality of the service* that I was getting at the dealer here in town, where I bought the car. The dealer I bring it to now *always* has the car ready when he says he will, and he does a *quality* job. For that, I don't mind the inconvenience of paying a little more and having the extra drive. Besides, he always *gives me a loaner* while the car's in the shop.

Now, let's list the criteria that the client provided:

> **well-made = quality**
> **fun**
> **sharp-looking = appearance**
> **family likes it = opinions of others**
> **don't want to take any risks = security**
> **always = dependable**
> **gives me a loaner = services**

Two or three other questions (about favorite restaurants and the like) can easily elicit additional criteria. *Note especially those criteria that appear several times in the client's answers on different topics.* It is a good idea to also ask questions about financial products (yours or a competitor's) that the client has purchased previously because they are now closely related to what you are trying to accomplish. In addition, while the client is answering these questions, you are also finding out about his psychological profile and his preference in sensory systems. Remember:

> **WE ALL HAVE CRITERIA THAT AFFECT MULTIPLE DECISIONS.**

Thus, if a person's primary motivations can be identified and listed in the order of importance to him, future sales presentations can be structured to address those pre-identified needs, desires, and motivations. Just take the features, benefits, and advantages of your product or service and predetermine how each would address a prime motivation of your client. There will probably be some overlap.

One way to practice eliciting clients' decisions-making criteria is to ask your friends or associates what they like about something (what doesn't matter). After asking the same person a few times about different things, you will notice that you are beginning to receive similar responses. The following discussion examines motivational equivalencies.

Motivational Equivalents

Although people tend to use consistent themes to make decisions, they rarely describe these themes using the same words all the time. For example, someone may go to a particular gas station because of the *large product line;* a particular clothing store because of *good selection;* a restaurant because of the *variety* of dishes on the menu. The same person may require *diversity* of interests in friends. In each case, the theme of available alternatives (the italicized words) was dominant. To sell to such a person, you would emphasize in your presentation the concept of multiplicity of choices by using synonyms that indicate choice.

Exhibit 19-3 lists some of the more common, or dominant, buying motivations, or themes, along with synonyms that can be used to describe them. The list is not exhaustive, but it will give you an idea of how synomyms can be used in the sales process. Remember, however, that while the "denotation," or dictionary definition, of a word is the same for everyone, the "connotation," or meaning, of the word will differ from individual to individual. It is extremely important to discover *exactly* what such words mean to your client. For example, *safety* means entirely different things to different investors; so does *risk* and *service*.

EXHIBIT 19-3
Key Buying Motivation Equivalencies

Advertising	Reputation	Name recognition	Familiarity
Alternatives	Variety	Selection	Product line
Appearance	Looks	Atmosphere	Ambiance
Cleanliness	Tidy	Neatness	Sanitary
Convenience	Location	Help	Service
Courtesy	Consideration	Service	Respect
Credit	Cash flow	Bargain	Discount
Dependability	Reliability	Reputation	Confidence
Extras	Gifts	Incentives	Bonuses
Habit	Tradition	Familiarity	Sentimental
Image	Style	Status	Prestige
Integrity	Honesty	Trustworthy	Honor/trust
Money	Price	Cost	Discount
Performance	Durability	Standards	Quality
Prestige	Class	Peer pressure	Status
Professional	Competent	Expert	Authority
Prompt	Quick	Speedy	Dependable
Quality	Value	Craftsmanship	Reliable
Relationship	Loyalty	Friendliness	Affiliation
Reputation	Referral	Popularity	Prestige
Safety	Security	Guarantee	Warranty
Service	Help	Assistance	Courtesy
Status	Prestige	Authority	Preeminence
Suitability	Appropriateness	Applicability	Relevance
Times open	Convenience	Long hours	Ease

THE ART OF
TELEPHONE PROSPECTING

As a financial consultant, you have only three ways to increase the amount of assets that you manage: making money for your clients, obtaining referrals, and prospecting. In today's financial market, you must prospect to survive. How you prospect will vary with the nature of your market. However, for most FCs, cold calling is the technique of choice for obtaining new clients. This section includes chapters on telephone prospecting, while Section Six discusses face-to-face prospecting and profiling. In all of these situations, the various rapport-building and information-gathering techniques presented in the previous sections can be put to good use.

CHAPTER 20

Prospecting Tips

Cold calling, face-to-face meetings, seminars, and mailings are just a few of the many ways to prospect. Regardless of how you prospect (whether you use just one or a combination of techniques), it is extremely important to be consistent. Establish a prospecting schedule and keep to it.

TOP PRODUCERS ARE CONSISTENT PROSPECTORS.

When to Prospect

One of the most difficult hurdles in prospecting business executives is getting past their screeners. The easiest single way to do this is to call when the screener is out. Most successful executives are in their office by eight o'clock (many are in by seven). Their screeners usually arrive at nine o'clock. During that unprotected hour or two, executives answer their own phones. The same is true after five o'clock in the afternoon. Most successful executives leave the office about six or seven, while their screeners leave at five. In order to reach these prospects, you should also come in early and be prepared to stay late. We suggest that you also work on Saturday mornings. A successful FC we know once reached all but one of Ford Motor Company's vice presidents at their desks on a Saturday morning.

If you wish to reach a prospect at home, try calling in the evening between seven and nine. Weekends are particularly effective for reaching people. Avoid calling after nine o'clock on week nights, and before ten in the morning on weekends. Making a bad first impression calling too early or too late doesn't help build rapport.

During normal business hours is the best time to call chief financial officers, comptrollers, and presidents of small companies to offer business financial services. These people are in the business of investing and protecting their company's daily cash flow. If you can help them save or make money, they can't afford not to talk to you. In your opener, make sure to mention your name, the name of your firm, and the fact that you are calling regarding business financial services (e.g., business lines of credit) rather than personal services. If you don't get through right away, they will usually call back.

Getting Through the Screener

There are many techniques for getting through screeners. Here are two that we feel are *critical to avoid:*

- Deceit
- Threats or abuse

Lying creates problems. To begin with, you will almost always be found out by the prospect. Would you invest large sums of money with someone whose first act in the relationship was a lie? Second, you will be making hundreds of prospecting calls each week. Any psychologist will tell you that it's impossible to lie several hundred times a week and not have it affect your relationships with yourself, your family, and your friends.

Threatening a screener (e.g., "If you don't let me speak to him, I'll have to hold you legally responsible for the financial results") is also very counterproductive. What would you do if your secretary told you that someone had threatened him or her or that the caller had been abusive? It is not uncommon for irate executives to call an FC's manager to complain about such tactics.

Always be respectful toward the screener. Most good screeners will not let you through, no matter what you do. Many are qualified prospects in their own right, however, and therefore should not be ignored. When calling a specific individual, state your name and firm and ask for the individual with whom you wish to speak. If that person is "not available" now, always leave your name, your firm's name, and a message. A remarkable number of prospects call back, and when they do, it is no longer a cold call because you know they are interested. Always leave your name and number with professionals (e.g., doctors, lawyers), since some will return calls.

Of course, where you are located in the country will have much to do with how easy it is to reach prospects and how willing they will be to talk. Regardless of where you are, call.

Goal Setting

Set yourself a daily cold-calling goal. (See Chapter 3, "Effective Goal Setting" for an in-depth discussion.) One hundred contacts a day is usually good for a start. Once you begin to make contact, you could also add a goal of one face-to-face meeting each day. Don't leave the office until you have met your goal. However, when you have met it, give yourself some small reward. The nature of the reward isn't important, but you'll be surprised at its effect. Simple self-motivation really works. To succeed, you will need to work at least two nights per week for your first three years in the business.

Cold calling involves a lot of rejection. It's important to realize that prospects are not rejecting you. They don't even know you! What they are doing is passing up the opportunity to have a professional manage their investments. The fact is that whenever you (a professional who puts the client first) call a prospect to offer your services, you are doing that person a favor. There are millions of qualified prospects who would be thrilled to have you manage their investments, if they only knew you existed. The reason you cold-call is to let them know that you do exist and to give them the opportunity of working with you. If they refuse, that's *their* problem.

Statistics from various studies done by major brokerage houses show that for every one hundred contacts, ten prospects will listen and go on to a second call or meeting. For every ten who go on to a second call, one will become a client. (Depending on the source of your prospects, you may get three to ten qualified clients from the one hundred contacts.) And these statistics are based upon research done on nonprofessionals who were *reading* scripts during the call. In a word, anyone willing to make one hundred contacts per day should develop an average of one new client each day.

Subsequent research has shown that if you strive to overcome initial resistance by prospects, you will triple the number of new accounts you open. Think about it: Even a mediocre FC can open between 250 and 700 new accounts a year just by dialing consistently and diligently trying to overcome initial resistance.

> ### CONSISTENT DIALING PAYS OFF.

Where to Find Qualified Lists

Below is a partial list of places where you can find the names of qualified prospects:

- Lists of names (these cost between 10 cents and 75 cents per name, and have already been sold to other brokers).
- Lists of contributors to charitable or political organizations.
- Country club membership lists.
- Membership lists of professional organizations.

- Alumni directories, especially for business and professional schools.
- *Cole's Directory* (a reverse telephone directory that gives addresses first and then the name and telephone number of the occupant).
- *The Directory of Directories* (can be found in the resource section of any sizable library; contains the costs of and the subscription addresses of any membership list in the country).
- Newspaper advertisements selling expensive cars.
- Recent real estate sales.

For additional sources of lists, see Appendix 2, page 283.

Account-Opening First Calls

During your sales career, you will be exposed to a variety of ways to prospect by phone, as well as several prospecting philosophies. The following approach, and the psychology behind it, have proved successful.

There are four things that you *must* accomplish during the prospecting call:

1. Qualify the prospect to determine whether you wish to pursue a relationship.
2. Begin a relationship with the now-qualified prospect.
3. Establish a benefit for the prospect for meeting with you (find a need that you can begin to fill during that meeting).
4. Set up the meeting.

(*Note:* Some people recommend selling something to the prospect on the first or second call. They feel that the purpose of finding a need in the first call is to set up that sale. We disagree. Remember that everything you do or say, or fail to do or say, communicates something to your client/prospect. Do you want to communicate that you "shoot from the hip"?

Clients we have polled have told us that if a financial consultant tries to sell them something on the second or, especially, the first call, they think the FC is only after a sale and not interested in them. We think that first- or second-call selling is not even professional. After all, how comfortable would you be with a doctor who prescribed a solution to your ailment after a brief telephone conversation, without examining you?

The Prospecting Track

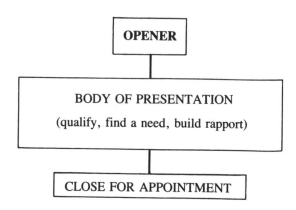

You can qualify the prospect by probing to determine if he has the needs and resources necessary to justify working with him. Once you decide that you wish to continue the relationship, it is important to court your prospective client. Do this by establishing rapport and piquing his interest in you, your firm, and your products and services.

You must convince your prospect that you and your firm are ready, willing, and able to help meet his financial needs. Finally, you must set up a second call or a face-to-face appointment. All of this generally has to be accomplished in the few minutes in which most people are willing to listen before they become impatient.

It is important to remember both the immediate and the ultimate objectives of the first cold call. The immediate goal is to qualify the prospect *and* to begin a relationship. The ultimate objective is to establish a long-term relationship that will be profitable to you both. To keep this in mind, it is useful to consider the call from the prospect's point of view.

**LONG-TERM RELATIONSHIPS ARE YOUR
ULTIMATE OBJECTIVE.**

There are very few people who sit by the phone thinking, "I hope a financial consultant gives me a call. Come on phone, ring! I want to buy something from somebody!" Consequently, almost by definition, your phone call is *always* an interruption! No matter how interesting your presentation, you are taking the prospect away from something he was already doing. When you think about it, you make a living by interrupting people.

Depending upon the area of the country in which you are located, such interrupting is more or less of a problem. In some areas (e.g., New York City), it is very important to complete the objectives of the call as quickly as possible (sometimes in as little as three to five minutes), because the dominant attitude is to "make it quick." Remember, though, a speeded-up approach often gives the impression of abruptness to natives of other areas.

Most notably in some parts of the South and West, people are usually more patient and will allow you time to develop the relationship. This enables you to obtain additional data that might be difficult to elicit during a first call in New York. Be aware of the cultural requirements and expectations of your area.

Use whatever time the prospect allows you to identify a key need and to develop rapport. The important thing is to be sure that you are sensitive to the cues given by the prospect so that you can suggest closing the call before he does.

Scripts

Whether or not you choose to script your prospecting presentations is up to you. However, have you ever been in the middle of the first call or a sales presentation, and reached for just the right word only to find it wasn't there? That has happened to most of us—but it doesn't have to.

If you were invited to speak about investments (or life insurance or banking) to the Chamber of Commerce in a major city, would you write out your speech beforehand or just ad lib? Nearly all of us would write out what we wanted to say so that we would gain the most impact in the fewest words. If that is true when speaking to a group of people, why shouldn't it be true when speaking to each of them individually?

By writing out what you want to say, you can carefully select just the right words to give your presentation exactly the flavor that you wish. Once you've double-checked your script to make sure that it's exactly as you want it, read it out loud a dozen times. This will help you to perfect the timing of your presentation and will form memory patterns in your brain. The next time you reach for just the right word, it will be there.

SCRIPTING IS JUST ANOTHER WORD FOR BEING PREPARED.

Profiles

Your prospects will display every type of emotional response to your call. Remember that you will generally be able to psychologically profile a prospect within the first sixty seconds of the call. Is he or she a Bureaucrat, a Dictator, an Executive, or a Socialite?

- *Bureaucrat prospects* are generally reticent about speaking, even when they are interested in your presentation. Don't give up simply because they don't give you a lot of encouragement.
- *Dictator prospects* may initially be somewhat intimidating. Use the CLAPing technique (see Chapter 7, ''Responding to Clients' Concerns'') to let them ventilate while you determine their needs.
- *Executive prospects* will usually give you time to make a well-organized presentation. In addition, if your opening does not

initially deal with an area they are interested in, they will frequently respond positively if you try to redirect the conversation toward eliciting their needs.

- *Socialite prospects* may provide far more information, and take up far more time than you are prepared to spend, on the first call. While they are the easiest prospects to talk to, remember that Socialites do not generally make firm commitments. You must determine how much time you wish to spend with them.

CHAPTER 22

Opening the Call

When calling a prospect for the first time, the purpose of your opening statement is to generate enough interest during the first few moments of the call to hold your prospect's attention for the next few minutes. Your initial statement is designed to bypass the automatic "No!" response that so many people seem to give instinctively to salespeople.

> **IF YOU CAN'T KEEP THE PROSPECT ON THE PHONE, YOU CAN'T MAKE HIM A CLIENT.**

There are three types of opening statements: (1) product-specific; (2) service-specific; and (3) generic. Each works for, each appeals to, specific personality types, and each has its advantages and disadvantages. Because different openers contain different levels of threat to a prospect, each will result in different levels of resistance on the client's part. The following pages provide examples of several types of openers, whom they appeal to among both FCs and prospects), and how threatening a prospect might consider them. (For additional openers, see Appendix 3, page 286.)

Product-Specific Openers

A product-specific opener is exactly what its name implies: calling prospects to determine whether they would be interested in buying a specific product or service. It is a hit-or-miss approach if you don't know what the client is interested in. On the other hand, if you are calling a prospect you *know* has an interest in or need for the product, it is the most powerful opener. For this opener to work most effectively, it is critical to pre-qualify prospects. One way to do this is to buy lists of people who have purchased that product before.

Product-specific openers appeal to aggressive FCs. Their chief advantage is that they elicit an immediate response so that the call ends quickly if the prospect is not interested. This is an important advantage and can result in a quick sale. Product-specific openers appeal to sophisticated prospects who meet three criteria:

1. They know what they want or "need."
2. They are interested in what you are currently selling.
3. They have the money to spend now.

THE PRODUCT-SPECIFIC OPENER IS THE RIFLE APPROACH TO PROSPECTING.

Some of the disadvantages of the product-specific opener are:

• They immediately identify you as a "salesperson" in the mind of the prospect. Once this mind-set has been established, it is almost impossible to change.

- Because of the sales bias of the approach, the product-specific opener can be very threatening to many prospects. This can, in turn, result in increased sales resistance on their part.
- This kind of opener does not work well with unsophisticated (inexperienced) buyers who do not understand your product or service and do not know exactly what they want.
- Although many FCs think otherwise, we have found that it can be very difficult to move from a product-specific opener to determining a prospect's overall needs. The prospect may think you are saying, "Since you don't want to buy this product, is there something else I can call back with to sell you later?"

(*Note:* Some neophyte FCs think cold calling sophisticated prospects is ideal because such a call often results in a quick sale and commission. However, sophisticated prospects rarely give any one broker more than a small percentage of their total assets, and they frequently know more than the new FC. In addition, they tend to quickly transfer their accounts when the market turns or someone else calls with a "better" new idea. Many new FCs appear to prospect almost exclusively for this kind of client and, after doing well initially, frequently lose many of their clients when the market turns because they never established a solid relationship.

The following are examples of product-specific openers:

> *FC:* Hello. This is _____, with Prudential Bache Securities. I'm calling with some information on our latest Municipal Investment Trust, number 614, which is currently yielding 8 percent tax free, paid monthly. Do you have a need for tax-free income?

> *FC:* Hello, this is _____, with Merrill Lynch. I'm calling the owners of sporting goods stores with information on our newest offering of stock in Reebock Athletic Shoes. If you sell Reebocks, I'm sure that you already know how well they are made and how quickly they are selling. Would you like to hear more?

> *FC:* Hello, this is _____, with Chase Manhattan Bank. I'm calling with some information on a new business line of credit that we're making available to professionals such as yourself. Do you currently have a line of credit for your business?

FC: Hello, this is ⎯⎯⎯⎯ , with the Metropolitan Life Insurance Company. I'm calling to introduce a new, low-cost term insurance designed to cover key employees of small corporations. Do you currently have key-employee insurance?

Service-Specific Openers

This type of opener is essentially the same as the product-specific opener. However, if the service with which you are calling is "free," prospects will perceive it as considerably less threatening. Examples of such free services are your firm's version of a cash management account or an IRA; free portfolio or tax analysis; and free retirement planning.

The service-specific opener appeals to FCs who have warm personalities and wish to establish rapport with the client for a longer-term relationship. It is appealing to prospects for the following reasons:

• Depending upon the service specified, more prospects may be able to see more quickly the benefits for themselves than they would with a product-specific opener.
• There is far less pressure to buy something. Incidentally, the second point makes it far easier for the FC to keep prospects on the phone to qualify them and build rapport.

Prospects' responses to the service-specific opener will depend upon their personality. We have listed the responses you can expect from four types of prospects:

• *Executive:* This kind of opener will generally lead to an excellent first call. Remember to organize your opening well and quickly elicit the Executive's needs while you are building rapport.
• *Socialite:* The service opener can result in a long prospecting call that provides a great deal of information. Unfortunately, it may accomplish little unless you maintain firm control of the call, because the Socialite frequently rambles.

- *Bureaucrat:* Because the service-specific opener is not threatening, this kind of call will frequently result in more involvement than a product-specific opener would. Involve the Bureaucrat early in the call with open probes.

- *Dictator:* The service-specific call addresses a broad, current need, without appealing to the Dictator's self-esteem needs. Hence, although it is nonthreatening to him, it may also fail to make intrigue him because it will not make him feel special. As a result, it may initially elicit a hostile response. This prospect may also respond with hostility because he perceives this opener as evidence of weakness, which could lead him to attempt to dominate the call.

    The Dictator prospect will often respond more positively if the service offered is one that appeals to his esteem needs—for example, any service oriented to a small group of elite individuals, such as premier accounts for the very successful. If he becomes hostile, use CLAPing techniques (see Chapter 7).

    Some disadvantages of the service-specific opener are:

- This opener does not carry as much "sizzle" as a product-specific opener.
- With a prospect's encouragement, some FCs succumb to the temptation to spend more time socializing than is effective.

The following two service-specific openers have proved effective:

> *FC:* Hello. This is _____, at Citibank. I'm calling to introduce our new cash management account. It provides more than twice the services as similar accounts at most other banks, and at lower cost to you. Do you currently have a cash management account?

> *FC:* Hello. This is _____, at Donaldson Lufkin and Jenrette. As April 15th approaches, I'm calling investors to determine if they currently have an IRA. Despite the recent changes in the tax laws, a great many people are still eligible to open and contribute to an IRA account before taxes. That can result in substantial tax savings while providing a nest egg for retirement. Do you currently have an IRA?

Generic Openers

The generic is the broadest of the openers. If the product-specific approach is like hunting with a rifle, the generic is like hunting with a shotgun. Its broader appeal makes it easier to hit more targets. It may refer to a wide range of products or services, or to a generic concept. This kind of opener is particularly useful if you are calling from a list that has not been prequalified for a specific product or service—for example, financial planning (the generic concept); your firm's broad range of banking, information, or insurance services; and information on the latest tax law changes.

Generic openers appeal primarily to warm FCs (both the leader and the follower types) because they are excellent means of establishing a relationship. The leader financial consultant likes them because they are a useful tool. The follower FC likes them because they are nonthreatening and less likely to result in rejection.

Because they tend to be nonthreatening, generic openers appeal to prospects in the same way that service-specific openers do. As long as you are able to come to the point and quickly demonstrate a benefit to your prospect, most people will listen. Generic openers are particularly useful in that they give you great flexibility in accomplishing a smooth transition from the original purpose of the call to identifying a more pertinent need of the prospect.

The generic, like the product-specific opener, can be a two-edged sword. We mentioned that the product-specific opener is not only the most exciting, but also the most threatening. Similarly, while generic openers are less threatening, they can also be the least exciting.

The advantages of the generic opener are fourfold:

• They enable you to present yourself as a professional who is calling to determine how you can help the prospect, rather than as a salesperson who is calling to determine how you can use him.

• Since generic openers are generally nonthreatening, they do not generate additional barriers to overcome in establishing rapport with the prospect.

- They provide an easy vehicle for qualifying the prospect and setting up future contacts in order to profile him and open the account.
- They focus the interaction on you and your firm. This enables you to project more of your personality to the prospect as you establish the relationship.

Despite its popular appeal, the generic opener does have certain disadvantages:

- You must move quickly to elicit a need and show that you can meet it. If you don't you may irritate or even alienate many prospects.
- The generic opener encourages FCs who are followers to talk too much.
- It may not be as exciting as a product-specific opener.

You should note that none of these disadvantages is inevitable if you can get the prospect talking.

THE GENERIC OPENER IS THE SHOTGUN APPROACH TO PROSPECTING.

EXAMPLES—GENERIC OPENERS:

FC: Hello. This _____, at Dean Witter. I'm calling to introduce our financial planning services. Essentially, this is a group of services that we have developed to help you plan for your retirement, your children's education, your taxes, and even—God forbid—your death or disability. Do you currently have a financial plan?

FC: Hello. This is _____, at Drexel Burnham Lambert. I'm calling with some information on the latest changes in the tax code and how they could affect your investments. Are taxes currently a concern for you?

Territorial Conflicts

If other FCs from your firm are calling the same people, it is important to avoid conflicts over accounts. If possible, the opener is the best time to find out if your prospect already has an account with your firm. After all, it is quite frustrating to find out halfway through a face-to-face meeting that your new "client" already has a FC from your firm.

You may find it useful to introduce yourself, your firm, and the purpose of your call in the opening.

EXAMPLE:

FC: Ms. Jones, this is John Doe with Merrill Lynch, and I'm calling with some information on the latest changes to the tax code and the effects they can have on your investments. *Are you familiar with us?*

This opener accomplishes two things:

1. It introduces you, Merrill Lynch, and your services.
2. It probes to determine whether your prospect already has an account at Merrill Lynch.

The question, "Are you familiar with us?" can be thought of as a logical non sequitur. Unconsciously, the prospect is expecting to be asked if he is familiar with the product or service that is the subject of the call, if you can continue, or if he has an account with your firm. All of these questions follow logically from the introductory sentence. However, the question, "Are you familiar with us?" is unexpected and sufficiently different to put the prospect off balance. It requires him to pause momentarily before answering. Experience has shown that 95 percent of the time, rather than answering with a flat "I'm not interested" or "I already have another sales representative," the prospect will indicate if he has an account with your firm. In addition, by answering the question, he will allow you to complete the body of the presentation.

After the opener, it is important to probe for information

relating to the prospect's financial interests or needs. This will determine whether you should continue with your original opener or expand into a different area by probing for additional needs.

Few prospects will be prepared to commit to anything during the opening of a call. Hence probing for commitment (even commitment to hear more of your idea) can be sufficiently threatening that the prospect will end the call at that point.

The probe for information is an important transition into the body of the call. It can lead into a series of probes regarding the prospect's qualifications and his needs and interests. It can also determine what service or product he needs.

Always remember to prepare in advance for the most common responses (positive and negative) that are expected to your opener (see Appendix 4, "Responses to Prospecting Stalls and Objections," page 290). Doing so will enable you to ease the transition into the body of your presentation and provide you with the flexibility you need to keep the prospect's interest while you determine his needs.

```
BE PREPARED FOR ANY RESPONSE.
```

One way to prepare yourself for any response is by scripting. Once you've selected an opener that fits your personality, write down the four or five responses you are most likely to get. Then write out your answer to each response. Next, write out the two or three most likely responses to your answers and then your answers to those. Be sure that each of these answers includes an effective transition into the body of the presentation. We have provided a flow chart for such a script in Exhibit 22-1.

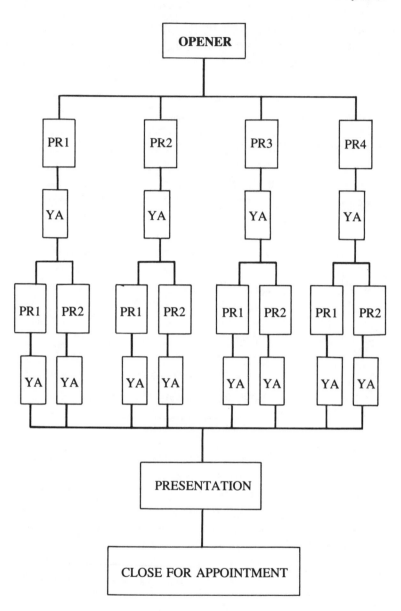

PR = PROSPECT'S RESPONSE   YA = YOUR ANSWER

CHAPTER 23

The Body of the Presentation

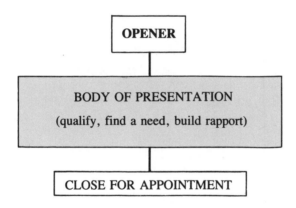

Once you have obtained your prospect's explicit or implied permission to continue your presentation, you must accomplish the following in the body of your call:

- Determine if the prospect is sufficiently qualified to justify making a second contact, either in person or on the phone.
- Determine a specific need or problem for which you can provide a solution.

- Lead the prospect to the conclusion that he wants to have additional contact to learn more about what you have to offer.
- Build sufficient rapport and trust so that the prospect will wish to learn about this product or service from you.
- Establish in the prospect the mind-set that you are a professional who may be able to help him.

Leading prospects to the conclusion that they wish to learn more consists of establishing a benefit (i.e., the solution of their needs problem).

EXAMPLE 1: You might use a financial planning opener. Mention that a great deal of interest in financial planning has been generated in the press in recent years. Almost everyone has read something on the topic, but most people have done nothing about it. The presentation should remind the prospect of the benefits of planning his finances, while also communicating that you have no desire to pressure him into "buying" anything.

EXAMPLE 2: If your prospect has indicated an interest in investments for his retirement fund, this not only enables you to discuss your firm's retirement-related products, but also provides an immediate rationale for probing for information regarding the investments and other actions that the prospect has already taken to prepare for retirement.

Building Rapport

Rapport building begins with the first words of the opener and continues throughout the relationship. It is important to use the skills of probing, pacing, and CLAPing discussed earlier. Always remember that you are a professional whose chief concern is the welfare of your client. If you do that, you will communicate your commitment to prospects and find that rapport comes much more easily. In addition, match your prospect's speech and emotional needs as determined by your psychological profile. Is she a Dictator, an Executive, a Socialite, or a Bureaucrat? Remember to make note of your client's sensory orientation and buying motivations.

Qualifying

The easiest and most ideal way to qualify prospects is to call from prequalified lists. However, this is not always possible. Moreover, even when you know that a prospect is qualified, there are two important reasons to ask some qualifying questions anyway:

1. It establishes and legitimizes a pattern of having the prospect answer questions that you ask (this becomes very important when profiling begins).
2. Every question the prospect answers inclines him to move psychologically closer to you and increases his emotional commitment to the relationship.

> **QUALIFYING QUESTIONS CAN HELP BUILD RAPPORT.**

We will deal with emotional commitment in more detail in Section Six. Here it is important to understand that every time a prospect answers a question, he makes himself increasingly open to you. He therefore also demonstrates an increase in the level of trust he has in you. To rationalize his new openness, the prospect must unconsciously justify his actions by attributing a level of trustworthiness and closeness to you that he would not normally do so quickly.

We cannot overstate the importance of using **open probes** as a tool in qualifying. By asking your prospect to speak freely about his interests and concerns, you demonstrate your interest and avoid the trap of appearing to interrogate him.

Few people appear to realize that **given the proper rationale, anyone will answer any question!** If you don't believe this, remember the questions you answered for your doctor the last time you got a physical examination. Getting a prospect to answer qualifying questions requires you to do only three things:

1. Demonstrate a benefit to him for answering the questions by tying them into the need or problem that you have elicited. For example: "Mr. Smith, my firm has several excellent financial-planning services available, depending upon the needs of the individual. Since I'm sure that you don't want to be bothered with several hundred pages of literature, would you mind if I asked you a few questions to determine which service would be most appropriate for you?

2. Use as few questions as possible to qualify the prospect. Make sure that you obtain the qualifying information that you need, but don't cut the prospect off prematurely.

3. Make your initial questions "safe"—that is, ask about matters that could be considered "public knowledge" relative to the need or problem that you are addressing—and then move on to more personal questions.

EXAMPLE 1: When using a financial-planning opener you might ask:

"Do you own your own home?"

"Are you a one- or a two-income family?"

"Do you have any children that you are planning to send to college?"

"Have you ever invested before, such as in certificates of deposit, money market funds, savings bonds, mutual funds, or stocks or bonds?"

"Tell me about them."

"What is your most important financial concern at this time: college, retirement, or something else?"

"Can you give me an idea of what your current income tax bracket is?"

EXAMPLE 2: If you had elicited a concern about the prospect's taxes, you might have begun with such questions as:

"Can you give me an idea of your greatest tax concern?"

"Is the alternative minimum tax a concern for you?"

"What sources of income do you have in addition to your salary?"

"What steps are you already taking to reduce your tax liability?"

"Are you currently working with someone regarding this problem?"

"How have your investments affected your tax liability?"

Notice how in the financial-planning example the FC begins by asking for information that the prospect's neighbors know, and then moves to a more personal level. In the tax example, the questions specifically probe tax-related problems. Remember, the questions you ask should always relate to the prospect's identified need or problem. Avoid getting locked into a single, rigid system of probes. (See Appendix 5, "Profiling Questions," page 294.)

GIVEN AN EFFECTIVE RATIONALE, ANYONE WILL ANSWER ANY QUESTION.

CHAPTER 24

Getting the Appointment: Closing the Prospecting Call

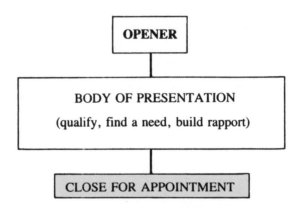

In a prospecting call, the close is a two-step process that: (1) establishes the rationale for future contact; and then (2) sets up a second call or a meeting. Again, it is necessary to establish the benefit of an additional contact to the prospect.

EXAMPLE:

FC: Ms. Jones, now that I have some idea of which plan would be most appropriate for you, I'd like to send you a brochure that will explain it in more detail. I'd also like to make an appointment to speak with you and your husband to answer your questions and discuss the plan in more detail.

This is beneficial to the prospect and still nonthreatening.

When setting up a second call, it is important to make it a business appointment. Many FCs become very frustrated when they make their second call and find that the prospect has forgotten about it. To decrease the chance of this happening, make an appointment for a business meeting by phone.

EXAMPLE:

> *FC:* Ms. Jones, I'll call back Tuesday night at seven to discuss your IRA with you. Thank you very much. This is John Doe with Shearson, and I look forward to speaking with you Tuesday night at seven. Good-bye.

Once you have established the time and agenda for the call, it is as important to call the prospect at that time as it is for you to arrive at a meeting on time. Promptness helps to establish you as trustworthy, competent, and professional.

As we demonstrated above, be sure to repeat your name and the name of your firm at the end of the call. And always remember to send any literature that you have promised.

The Pros and Cons of Sending Literature

It is worth noting that some financial consultants feel sending literature is a waste of time and money. We have compiled a list of some potential advantages and disadvantages.

The potential advantages of sending literature are:

- The literature gives prospects something tangible with your name and your firm's name on it. It also proves that you are not someone trying to determine if they are worth robbing.
- It is possible that the prospect will read it (a surprising number do).
- A professional does what he says he will do (if you promise it, send it).

The potential disadvantages of sending literature are:

- Sales literature is expensive and takes time to put together for mailing each day.
- Some sales literature is very complex and may confuse prospects, thereby becoming a barrier to future contact.

> **SCREEN YOUR PRODUCT/SERVICE LITERATURE BEFORE SENDING IT.**

Carefully screen the literature that you intend to send to determine whether it may confuse your prospect. If you believe that it is sufficiently supportive of what you are trying to accomplish, send it. If you believe that it is too complicated, but still feel a need to send it, discuss it with the prospect first. Explain that the literature may be confusing and give a brief explanation of what it says before you close the call. Offer to explain the material again and to answer any questions that the prospect has when you call or see him again. Finally, be sure the prospect understands that there is no reason to feel embarrassed if the material confuses him or raises questions in his mind. In so doing, you demonstrate your value as a professional who can help him meet his needs or problem.

Asking for Referrals

We think it is best to wait until later in the relationship to ask for referrals. On the first call you have not done anything for the prospect and thus have not given him sufficient reason to recommend you to others. As a result, we suggest waiting until the completion of a sales call or the profiling meeting to seek referrals.

There is an *exception* to the above rule: If the prospect is "not interested," ask if he knows anyone who might be interested. We know of one enterprising young FC who, when told by a prospect that he wouldn't do business with that firm if it were the last one on earth, asked the prospect if he would give the name of his worst competitor. The prospect laughed and gave the FC the name. When the FC called the referral and told him how he had gotten his name, he was invited to make a presentation and obtained a new client. The FC, of course, called the original prospect back and thanked him for the referral. When the prospect heard that his biggest competitor had opened an account with the FC, he, too, invited him to make a presentation. In the end, the FC obtained two corporate accounts where he would have received none if he had failed to ask for a referral.

Summary

Thus far, in this section, we have provided a series of suggestions to increase the effectiveness of your prospecting presentations. The next chapter furnishes an example of a generic script for financial planning services in the format that we have suggested.

The Prospecting Script

To help you write a prospecting script using our recommended format, we have provided an example of such a script in this chapter. It is a generic script that might be used to sell financial planning services.

Generic Script: Financial Planning Services

FC: May I speak to (*prospect's name*), please? How are you? This is (*your name*) at (*your firm*), calling with some information on our financial planning services. Are you familiar with us?

Prospect: Yes.

FC: Wonderful! Essentially, these are a group of services that we've put together to help you plan for your taxes, retirement, kids' education, or even, God forbid, death or disability. Do you currently have a financial plan?

Prospect: 1. Yes.

       2. No.

       3. I'm not interested.

       4. I already have a broker.

EXHIBIT 25-1
The Prospecting Track

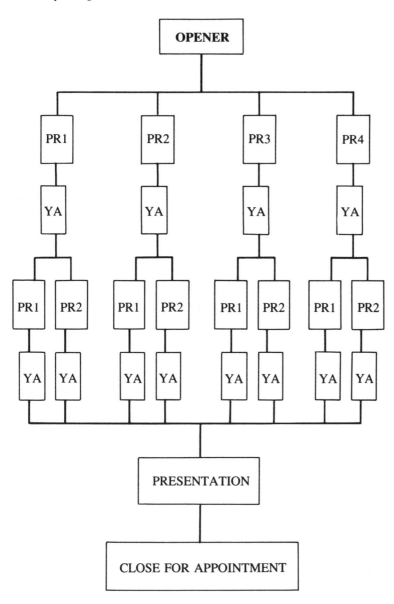

PR = PROSPECT'S RESPONSE   YA = YOUR ANSWER

If the prospect does have a financial plan (response #1):

FC: That's great! It's so nice to finally speak with someone who is actually doing something about their future. Considering the latest changes in the tax, retirement, and estate laws, not to mention the changes in college tuition, may I ask if it's been updated recently?

Prospect: 1a. Yes.

1b. No.

FC response to 1a: Very good! Then, based upon the results of your plan, may I ask what your chief investment concern is at this time—your retirement, your taxes, or your children's education?

Having identified a need, continue to build rapport and qualify the prospect.

[Rationale for asking questions.]

FC response to 1b: In that case, can you afford to continue to invest for your future based upon a plan that may very well be out-of-date? Here at (*your firm*), we can review your current plan and either update the areas where changes in the law will affect you or, if necessary, develop a completely new plan for you. May I ask you just a few questions to determine what your plan currently covers?

Prospect: Yes **or** What kind of questions?

[Examples of qualifying questions used by FC; for more qualifying/profiling questions, see Appendix 5.] [If necessary, give examples: CDs, money market funds, savings bonds, real estate, or even stocks and bonds.]

FC: For example, does your current plan tell you how much money you need to save each year in addition to your retirement benefits at work and your Social Security if you are to attain the life-style you desire when you retire? Does it take into account the changes in the retirement laws for your IRA and Keogh accounts? Do you have a Keogh account? Was it reviewed to check its performance record? (*Your firm*) can do that free. Do you have children or grandchildren that you are planning on putting through college? I'm sure that, together, we can determine approximately what it will cost to send your child to college when the time comes. Then we can determine what steps you need to take to prepare. Are taxes a concern for you? In what way? May I ask what steps you have taken to solve your tax concern? Are your current investments a concern, especially in light of the changes in the capital gains laws? May I ask what kinds of investments you have made?

Once qualified close for an appointment. Send the prospect your financial planning brochure and a list of materials that he will need to bring with him.

> *FC: (Prospect's name)*, I'd like to suggest that we meet and review your current plan so we can determine what, if anything, we can do to help you. May I suggest that you and your wife/husband come in for an appointment later this week? When you come in, bring your current plan and we'll review it quickly to see what needs to be done. We might even be able to do a few things while you're here. Then, if necessary, we can set up another appointment to update specific material. How does that sound?
>
> *Prospect:* Fine.
>
> *FC:* Great! How does *(day)* at *(time)* o'clock sound for you?
>
> *Prospect:* Fine.
>
> *FC:* Good! I'll see you and your wife/husband on *(day)* and at *(time)* o'clock to review your financial plan. That will take about thirty minutes. Our address is *(your address)*. This is *(your name)* at *(your firm)*. I look forward to seeing you then.

If the prospect does not have a financial plan (response #2):

> *FC:* Mr./Ms. *(prospect's name)*, would you mind if I asked you just a few questions? Maybe we can determine whether a financial plan is appropriate for you. Is retirement a concern for you? A recent survey indicated that only 3 percent of retired people are happy with their retirement arrangements. That's because most people spend more time planning for their three-week vacation each year than they do for their retirement. At *(your firm)*, if you can tell us what lifestyle you'd like when you retire, we can look at your retirement plan from work, your IRA/Keogh, and the Social Security you can expect, and tell you how much you need to begin saving *now* to achieve your goal. Do you have a Keogh account? Was it reviewed to check its performance record? *(Your firm)* can do that free. Do you have children or grandchildren that you are planning on putting through college?

[Provides a rationale for asking questions.]

Once the prospect has been qualified, close for an appointment. Send the prospect your financial planning brochure, and a list of materials that he will need to bring with him.

If the prospect said he was not interested (response #3):

> *FC:* All right. But before I let you go, I wonder if you could help me understand something. Our surveys show that only 3 percent of those retiring are happy with their retirement. They also show that most people spend more time planning their vacation each year than they do planning for their retirement or their children's education. Are you satisfied that your current plans will achieve your goals for your retirement and your children's education?
>
> *Prospect:* 3a. Yes.
>
>   3b. No.
>
> *FC response to 3a:* That's great! As you may know, (your firm) has the widest range of financial services available today to help you make that plan a success. May I ask what your number-one priority is? Retirement, taxes, or your children's education? And what steps have you already taken to achieve your goal? What's your second priority? And the steps for that?

By now the prospect should be effectively qualified. Close for an appointment.

> *FC response to 3b:* Has someone completed a formal financial plan for you? If you have just a moment, perhaps we can determine what areas you might wish to explore further. Is retirement a concern for you? A recent survey indicated that only 3 percent of retired people are happy with their retirement arrangements . . . (etc.)

Once the prospect is qualified, close for an appointment. Send the prospect your financial planning brochure and a list of materials that he will need to bring with him.

If the prospect already has a broker (response #4):

> *FC:* That's great! It's so nice to finally speak with someone who is really looking after their investments. Listen, before I go, (*your firm*) is taking a little survey. Could I ask you just one

question? The last time you and your broker met for your quarterly review of your investment plan, did you discuss the latest changes in the tax laws and the impact they will have on your investments?

Prospect: 4a. Yes.

4b. No.

FC response to 4a: It sounds as if you are very well taken care of. Can you think of anyone else whose investment future I might be able to help plan?

FC response to 4b: As you know, Congress has recently made dramatic changes in the way your investments, and even your estate, will be taxed. These changes affect everything from capital gains to municipal bonds and trust accounts for your children. Even real estate investments have been radically affected. What I'd like to do is send you some information that (your firm) has put together on these changes and then meet with you to discuss them in greater detail. Would that be all right?

Prospect: Yes.

FC: Good. Now, rather than overwhelm you with mounds of material that you don't need, may I ask you a few questions so that I can send you only materials that are specific to your interests?

Prospect: Fine.

FC: Good. To begin with, what is your greatest tax concern at this time? What steps have you already taken to solve it?

Prospect: (Response.)

FC: Very good. Are you subject to the alternative minimum tax? (Etc.)

Once the prospect is qualified, close for an appointment. Send the prospect your financial planning brochure and a list of materials that he will need to bring with him.

Self-evaluation

It is useful to periodically tape-record a prospecting call and study it to discover your strengths and the areas in which you need to improve. (*Note:* Check with your office manager regarding the legal ramifications of taping in your state.) Even if you tape only your end of the conversation, you'll learn a great deal when you listen to yourself. In Appendix 6, (see pages 300 to 303) we have provided examples of self-evaluation forms for both prospecting and sales calls. Make it a habit to evaluate the quality of your calls at least twice a week.

PROFILING

Why Profile?

There are several reasons for profiling a prospect or client, not the least of which is the information it provides. The New York Stock Exchange and various insurance and banking authorities require you to "know your client" before making recommendations for appropriate action. Failure to adequately profile a client not only makes it very difficult to determine the type and quantity of product most appropriate for him, but also leaves you vulnerable to a lawsuit if your recommendation does not perform as your client had hoped.

Some FCs wait until they have had a client on the books for months and have made several sales before they profile him. We think this does not make sense. In addition to the reasons provided above, profiling can be an excellent way to build the rapport and the trust necessary to

• convince the prospect to open an account, or

• encourage an existing client to transfer a larger portion of his assets to your care.

Obviously, there is nothing wrong with doing a further in-depth profile *after* a client has been on your books for a while. This can turn up a need for further planning or specific planning needs such as a different product or service. In fact, every contact with a client should be used to update your information on his situation.

It has been our experience that many FCs never adequately examine the clients that they do profile. As a result, when they ask clients about their investments or their financial situation, the clients' responses are not indicative of their true status (i.e., they don't tell "the truth, the whole truth, and nothing but the truth" about their finances). This makes it very hard to determine what size order you can ask for.

Asking for too small an order can make you look like "small potatoes" in your client's eyes, thereby resulting in the loss of hard-earned commission dollars when your client gives his big orders to his other FC(s). At the same time, asking for a big order can increase your production, but will not always be appropriate. By utilizing the psychological, communications, and rapport-building skills already discussed, the profiling techniques provided in this section will help you to avoid both traps and to obtain your client's complete financial status when you profile.

CHAPTER 26

How to Profile Effectively

Throughout the book, we have stressed the importance of stepping into your client's world so that you can sell to him from his point of view. Indeed, this is the essence of consultative selling and begins the moment you first make contact with a prospect. Formal profiling is just one way of gaining information regarding your prospect's or client's needs.

When to Profile

During your sales career, you have probably been exposed to several techniques for profiling. Most are excellent, and we suggest that you choose the one you are most comfortable with and use it or modify it to your needs. Regardless of your method, **always profile!** Profiling is one of the keys to long-term success.

> **PROFILE—THE CAREER YOU SAVE WILL BE YOUR OWN!**

Profiling begins with the qualifying questions you ask a prospect during a cold call. It continues through follow-up calls and your first face-to-face meeting. When properly done, profiling can become a habit that will continue throughout your relationship with the client. It also lets you update information on file with almost every contact.

Profiling During Follow-up Calls

Profiling during follow-up calls should accomplish three things:

1. It should elicit additional information regarding the prospect's interests, needs, and sophistication.
2. It should further qualify the prospect.
3. It should help lead the prospect to the conclusion that he needs to meet with you personally to discuss his situation more fully.

Begin each follow-up call by bridging to the preceding conversation and previously elicited needs. You should then deal with questions that have been generated by whatever literature you sent earlier. Next, move to questions that will provide additional details on the prospect's investment history. Remember that detailed, "threatening" questions are not necessary at this point. You can ask those kinds of questions more effectively in person.

Once you've obtained sufficient new information to justify the call and the need for a face-to-face meeting, set up the meeting. If you can give a sufficient benefit for meeting with you, the client will agree to do so.

Profiling Face-to-Face

As a tool for building rapport, meeting a prospect face-to-face cannot be overestimated. When "meeting" someone over the phone, you have to project your entire image through a single medium—your voice. This forces your prospect to imagine what you look like. It also makes it much harder for you to overcome any biases he or she may have regarding brokers.

It is much easier to communicate your interest and professionalism face-to-face. In the same way, it is much easier for a client to establish trust with someone he has met than with a faceless voice. Would you make a large purchase from a stranger talking to you over the phone?

The first few minutes of the face-to-face meeting should be directed toward building rapport and setting the client at ease. This is also a good time to reinforce the benefit of profiling. (Use the series of tools we discussed in Section Four to accomplish this.)

Profiling, like qualifying, begins with questions that are very general and nonthreatening, such as information that is basically public knowledge. If most of these questions have already been asked during the cold call, review the answers with the prospect before moving on. Then move toward obtaining the more personal, less public information. Remember that each question the prospect answers makes it easier for him to answer your next question. This is true because each time he answers a question, he makes himself more vulnerable to you. To justify this, he unconsciously leans toward you with his emotions and rationalizes that he trusts you.

After explaining why you will do so, take notes of the client's answers and represent them graphically. Some financial consultants like to use special profiling forms, but this can be threatening to some prospects. How did you like filling out your last medical history? We like to write freehand, using the pyramid form shown in Exhibit 26-1. Exhibit 26-2 shows a completed pyramid.

Place the prospect's current investments within the pyramid, including each investment's level of safety and its relationship to the overall asset mix. Then discuss with the client the appropriateness of each current holding relative to his stated goals and risk tolerance. If the goals, risks, and investments match, congratulate the client. If they don't CLAP (Clarify, Legitimize, Acknowledge, Probe) to determine if you have misunderstood his goals or risk tolerance. If there has been no misun-

EXHIBIT 26-1
Client Profile

List the prospect's/client's: ○ Assets and liabilities ○ Income flow ○ Insurance needs In the pyramid, place the client's current investments to show him their relationship to his overall risk tolerance.	*Write the prospect's/client's:* ○ Goals Add these parameters for each goal: (a) Steps already taken? (b) Risk tolerance? (c) % rate of growth? (d) % rate of income? (e) $ amount to invest?

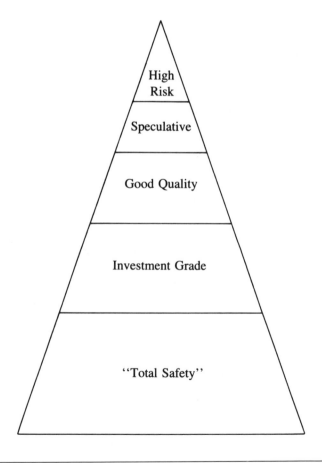

EXHIBIT 26-2
Sample Client Profile

William J. Donovan
Mary S. Donovan
4223 Excel Dr.
Butane, SD
Phone: 555-1212

Buying Criteria:
Safety
Convenience
Generally does not like stocks (with exception of IBM)
Note: Both generally "visual," "executives."

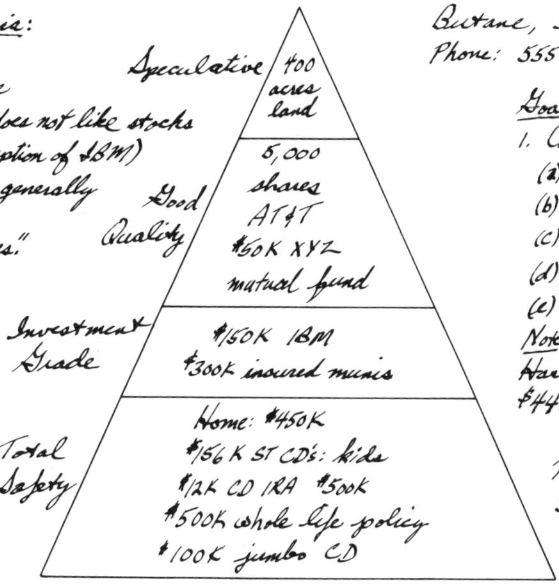
Speculative
400 acres land
Good Quality
5,000 shares AT&T
$50K XYZ mutual fund
Investment Grade
$150K IBM
$300K insured munis
Total Safety
Home: $450K
$156 K ST CD's: kids
$12K CD IRA $500K
$500K whole life policy
$100K jumbo CD

Goals:
1. Children's education:
   (a) $52K/child – 6 mo CDs
   (b) Investment grade, safety
   (c) Growth ≥ 9%/yr.
   (d) Income ≥ 9%/yr.
   (e) $200K for education
   Note: Wants children to attend Harvard. Will need approx. $440K for kid's education.
   Billy: 6 y.o. (12 yrs. to save)
   Mary: 4 y.o. (14 yrs. to save)
   Sally: 2 y.o. (16 yrs. to save)

2. Retirement:
   (a) Keogh—$250K ($150K in IBM stock, $100K jumbo CD)
   (b) IRA—Bill. $12K in zero coupon CDs maturing in 2000

3. Taxes:
   (a) $300K: $100K each in 3 different, insured, LT muni bonds

Assets:
Home: $450K
Stocks: 5,000 shares AT&T
$150K IBM
Mutual funds: $50K XYZ
Various munis and CDs (see pyramid)
Investment property: 400 acres raw land

Insurance:
$500 K renewable term each
$500 K Bill whole life
$10 MYN liability
Home, car, kids, and disability are covered.
Note: Has not insured against estate taxes.

Liabilities:
Owes $75K for home mortgage
No other liabilities

Personal:
Bill, partner in law firm
Mary does not work
Ages: Bill 42
Mary 40

derstanding, you have just demonstrated to your prospect your professionalism. You may also have just earned your first trade.

After you have elicited the prospect's goals, probe to determine the parameters of each goal. In dealing with investments, you need to know:

- What steps the prospect has already taken to meet his goal? (This will tell you what investments he has made without your having to ask specifically for that information.)
- How safe the investment must be (the prospect's risk tolerance for *this* goal).
- How quickly the investment must grow (level, or percent, of compounding necessary).
- Whether the client will require current income from the investment? (How much [percent]?)
- How much the client wishes to invest in a solution to this goal and when he wishes to invest it (he may not have those funds yet).
- Whether there are any types of investments that he wishes to avoid.

Armed with this information, it is relatively easy to find an appropriate investment to meet the prospect's needs.

Having represented your prospect's entire financial situation in graphic form, you should review it with him to verify its correctness and to make sure that he understands it. The review accomplishes two things:

1. For most people, this will be the first time that they have ever seen a single representation of their situation in graphic form.
2. As you review the parameters of each goal, your prospect will be committing himself (unconsciously) to act upon any solution that meets those parameters.

Before parting, make a copy of the representation and give the original to your prospect. It represents a plan that the two of you together have effectively made to meet his goals.

Once you have reviewed the representation with the prospect, discuss **generic** solutions to the problems. Include the approximate dollar amounts that the prospect wishes to spend to achieve each goal. In doing so, you both presell any investment or service for which you will later call and ensure that the amount of each order you ask for will be appropriate! Once you have finished this review, it is up to you to complete the necessary new account forms before the client leaves.

Remember the Chicago Board Options Exchange survey that we mentioned earlier (see page 10)? We think it is worth the consideration of all FCs. The CBOE found that if you place a client in only one kind of investment (e.g., stocks), you have only a 33 percent chance of keeping him for the next year. If you place him in two kinds of investments (e.g., stocks and bonds), you have a 67 percent chance of keeping him for the next year. But if you place your client in three or more types of investments (e.g., stocks, bonds, and insurance), you have an 83 percent chance of keeping him. The reasons for this are:

- The broader the product mix, the greater the professionalism you demonstrate, and hence the greater the client's dependence upon you for advice and support.
- The broader the product mix, the less likely you are to be affected by negative economic events (such as a major market or interest rate move).

Remember the old 80-20 rule: Most "successful" FCs obtain 80 percent of their revenue from 20 percent of their clients. However, when asked for additional information on the other 80 percent, many tell us that *they have only profiled 20 percent of their clients.* In addition, they did not receive their first large order from those clients until they had *met* them. The question is: Why didn't they make the effort to meet and profile all of their clients?

EXAMPLE: We know of a very successful broker who was promoted to management in his firm. Just before he entered management training, he distributed his accounts to the other FCs in the office. To one new man, he gave Mrs. X, an elderly lady for whom he had bought a $100,000 certificate of deposit.

"She's fully invested," said the broker. "But at least the account will increase your assets."

The young FC thanked him and the broker left for management training. When he returned, the young FC ran up to him and dropped on his knees to thank him, practically kissing his feet. At first, he assumed that this was merely respect for his new position as sales manager. However, when he asked, the new FC told him he wanted to thank him for the account that he had given him.

"What account?" he asked.

"Mrs. X. Last month we did $60,000 of production in her account, and this month we should do even more."

"Are you crazy?" asked the new sales manager. "You'll go to jail."

"Not at all," replied the FC. "Didn't you know that when she told you that she was fully invested, she thought that $12.5 million dollars in a money market fund was an investment. When I profiled her, we determined what her goals were, and we've made several investments to help her radically reduce her taxes."

The new sales manager had to be sedated.

> **PROPER PROFILING PRODUCES PROFIT!**

THE SALES TRACK

Some FCs prefer to sell by telephone, while others prefer to sell in person. If your manager or the nature of your relationship with your clients requires you to sell in a specific way, please continue to do so. However, if your sales method is up to you, examine the following comparison of telephone and in-person selling.

Selling by Phone versus Selling in Person

- Selling by phone is more efficient. It can save you time, travel, and expense. You can frequently make up to ten telephone sales in the time it would take to make one in-person sales call.

- Telephone sales are convenient. You can make the sale from any location that has a telephone. In addition, if you are calling from your office, you may have all the data available to answer the client's questions. If you are in the client's office, you must rely upon what you've brought with you.

- In-person sales are more personal. Whether in your office or your client's, in-person sales enable you to use all of your rapport-building and selling skills.

- If your product is complex, or must be demonstrated (e.g., certain forms of insurance and limited partnerships), you can't really sell it effectively by phone. (*Note:* The exception is if your client already has experience with the product and wants additional units.)
- Some markets are such that you must sell in person to maintain your client base. (Most insurance is sold face-to-face.) Also, in some countries in Europe and South America, securities can only be sold in person.
- If you sell in person, always call first to make an appointment. In addition to being courteous, this guarantees that your client will be there and ready to listen when you arrive.

Regardless of how you sell, the presentation itself consists of four parts that will be covered in the following chapters. The sales call follows the same four steps as a prospecting call (see Chapters 22, 23, and 24). With a few subtle differences, these are:

- Opening
- Body of the presentation
- Close
- Follow-up (which includes eliciting referrals)

The following exhibit diagrams the sales track.

EXHIBIT
The Sales Track

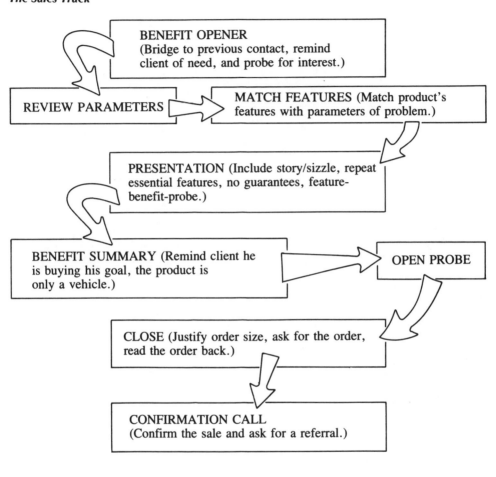

CHAPTER 27

The Opening

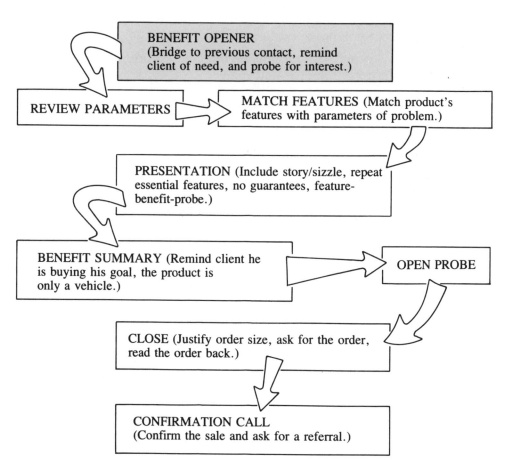

BENEFIT OPENER
(Bridge to previous contact, remind client of need, and probe for interest.)

REVIEW PARAMETERS

MATCH FEATURES (Match product's features with parameters of problem.)

PRESENTATION (Include story/sizzle, repeat essential features, no guarantees, feature-benefit-probe.)

BENEFIT SUMMARY (Remind client he is buying his goal, the product is only a vehicle.)

OPEN PROBE

CLOSE (Justify order size, ask for the order, read the order back.)

CONFIRMATION CALL
(Confirm the sale and ask for a referral.)

The first few moments of the sales call are perhaps the most important, yet most misused, part of the call. They communicate your agenda to your client. A remarkable number of sales are lost during this time because the FC fails to choose words based upon the client's point of view. Hence, instead of leading the client toward closing the sales, the FC begins by building an additional barrier between himself and the client.

Remember that any unscheduled sales call interrupts your client. Because of this, your opener must accomplish several things:

- It must remind your client of who you are.
- It must provide a rationale for the call that creates enough interest for the client to want to continue the call. (This is accomplished by reminding him that he has a financial problem, and that you have a solution).
- It must probe to determine if your client is prepared to deal with the purpose of call at that time.

Reminding your client of your relationship and the purpose of the call is relatively easy. Use a bridging statement to connect the current call to an earlier discussion of his needs.

EXAMPLE:

> *FC:* Mr. Smith, this is John Brown at Paine Webber. The last time we spoke, you mentioned an interest in increasing your retirement nest egg. [*Reminds the client of who the FC is and bridges to an earlier statement.*] Is this still your primary interest? [*Probes for validation of FC's assumption of the client's goal.*] I think I may have found just what you're looking for. [*I have a solution to your problem.*] Do you have a minute? [*Probes for acceptance.*]

(*Note:* If you will be making the sale in person, close here by setting up the time and place of the meeting.)

There are several ways to open a sales call. One of the most common, and least effective, is to start with a series of product features. Many FCs do this because they confuse the nature of features and benefits. This is an easy mistake to make, especially if you are just starting out. Our definitions of features and benefits, which reflect how they will be used throughout this book, are presented below.

FEATURE: A characteristic of a product, such as its price, growth, and expected dividend or interest payment. A feature remains a feature regardless of who buys the product. An example is the interest rate of a certificate of deposit.

BENEFIT: The ultimate purpose for which the client is buying the product—for example, using interest from a certificate of deposit to pay for retirement or a child's college tuition. In this example, the rate of interest is a feature. Retirement or the child's tuition is the benefit.

Advantages of Benefit Openers

The primary advantage of the benefit opener derives from the fact that the opener tells the client your objective. When you use a benefit opener, you tell the client that the primary purpose of your call is to help her achieve her goal (e.g., college tuition). For example:

> *FC:* Ms. Jones, the last time we spoke, you mentioned that your primary objective was obtaining sufficient funds to pay for John's college tuition. Is that still the case?

This reminds the client that you are a professional who has called to help her solve a problem (namely, affording her son's tuition), rather than a salesperson calling to solve your own problem (i.e., higher production credits). This difference is the reason why benefit openers create far less sales resistance than nonbenefit openers.

Disadvantages of NonBenefit Openers

The chief disadvantages of using a nonbenefit opener is its tendency to elicit unwanted sales resistance before you even begin your presentation. This happens because nonbenefit openers can confuse clients and tell them that you've only called to sell them something.

NONBENEFIT OPENERS BUILD SALES RESISTANCE.

Below are several examples of nonbenefit openers, followed by alternative benefit openers.

EXAMPLE 1: If you are selling stocks:

Nonbenefit:

> *FC:* Ms. Jones, this is John Doe at Prudential Bache Securities. How are you? The last time we spoke you said you wanted to invest in a good-quality growth stock. [*This clearly communicates the sales nature of the call.*]

Benefit:

> *FC:* Ms. Jones, this is John Doe at Prudential Bache Securities. How are you? The last time we spoke, you indicated that your primary concern was saving for your *children's education.* Is that still the case? [*Tells the client that you are calling to help her solve her tuition problem.*]

EXAMPLE 2: If you're involved in banking services:

Nonbenefit:

> *FC:* Mr. Black, this is Bob Smith at Chase Manhattan Bank. How are you today? The last time we spoke, you said that you had a $25,000 certificate of deposit coming due at your bank this Friday. [*This clearly indicates to the client that the purpose of the call is to invest his $25,000 for him.*]

Benefit:

> *FC:* Mr. Black, this is Bob Smith at Chase Manhattan Bank. How are you today? The last time we spoke, you said that your

chief concern was generating *enough income to live on* now that you are retired. Is that still the case? [*Tells the client that you may be able to help him obtain more income to live on.*]

EXAMPLE 3: If you are selling insurance:

Nonbenefit:

FC: Mrs. Johnson, this is Bill Jones at Metropolitan Life. How are you? Last week you mentioned that you only had $100,000 life insurance coverage. Is that still the case? [*Tells the client that you want to sell her life insurance, for your benefit.*]

Benefit:

FC: Mrs. Johnson, this is Bill Jones at Metropolitan Life. How are you? Last week you mentioned that you were concerned about how to protect your children's education in the event of your death. Is that still the case? [*Tells the client that you are ready to help ease her concern.*]

EXAMPLE 4: If you are selling instruments like mutual funds:

Nonbenefit:

FC: Mr. Brown, this is Phil Malloy at First Investors. How are you? When we last spoke, you said you had $20,000 coming due that you would like to invest in a mutual fund. Is that still the case? [*Tells the client that this is a sales call and that your primary interest is in getting to his $20,000.*]

Nonbenefit:

FC: Mr. Brown, this is Phil Malloy at First Investors. How are you? When we last spoke, you said that you would like to invest in a mutual fund. Is that still the case? [*While this is a far more effective approach, it still tells the client that the purpose of the call is sales. It also leads to at least some unconscious resistance—remember your resistance when the salesperson approached you in the store.*]

Benefit:

> *FC:* Mr. Brown, this is Phil Malloy at First Investors. How are you today? When we last spoke, you said that you wanted to fund your retirement in a way that would provide both current income and a hedge against inflation. Is that still the case? [*Reminds the client of the specific nature of his problem and implies that you have a solution.*]

Since the first things you mention communicate what you're most interested in, you have to decide if you want to create the impression that you are calling solely because you want to make a sale or because you are interested in helping the client. In reality, each of the openers above could be used by an FC whose only concern is the client's best interests, but the nonbenefit openers create a vastly better impression.

BENEFIT OPENERS REACH CLIENTS.

Need for Probes

It is as important to probe during the opener as it is to do so during the rest of the sales call. Only by probing throughout the call can you elicit confirmation of goals, assent to continue, and commitment to participate. Involve your client in the call as early as possible.

CHAPTER 28

Presenting Solutions to Your Client's Needs

Review the Parameters

One of the most important steps in profiling is eliciting the parameters of each of your client's goals or problems. Before you close the profiling meeting, you should review the parameters of each problem with the client, thereby accomplishing three things:

1. You verify your data.
2. You show the client that you were listening.
3. You commit the client to buy anything that meets or exceeds his parameters.

In other words, you presell the product or service that you will present later.

After you have completed your opener and received permission to continue with your presentation, begin the actual sales presentation by reviewing the parameters of the problem you've been asked to solve.

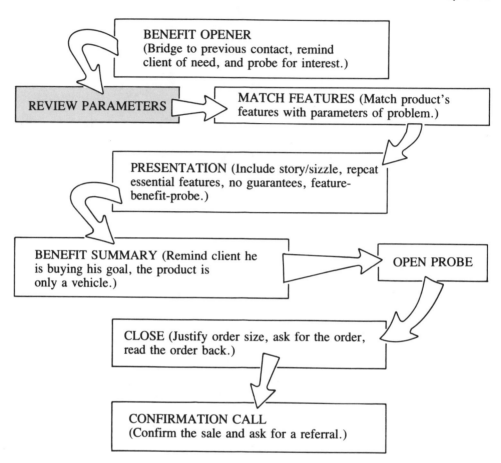

(*Note:* When selling in person, this would constitute the beginning of the face-to-face presentation.) This accomplishes several things:

- It begins the "yes set." The "yes set" is a technique in which you continually probe to verify that you and the client are on the same track. In addition, every time the client says "yes," he moves closer to a commitment.

- It shows the client that you are primarily interested in meeting his needs, rather than in just making the sale.

- It verifies to the client that you heard him correctly when he gave you the parameters of his problem, further demonstrating your interest.
- It verifies to you that your client hasn't changed the parameters, so you don't waste your time trying to sell a solution that is no longer appropriate.

We have used a buy-sell insurance scenario to illustrate how to review the parameters of your client's need. The client's profile indicates that he is a partner in a small business, an Executive personality type, who communicates primarily in the auditory mode:

FC: Mr. Rogers, this is Adam Schrum at Mutual of Omaha. How are you today?

Client: Fine, thank you.

FC: Great! The last time we *spoke,* you *stated* that you needed to find a way to protect your business in the event that either you or your partner should die. Is that still the case?

Client: Yes, it is.

FC: I think I may have the solution to your problem. Do you have a moment to *hear* about it?

[Probes for commitment to listen now.]

Client: Yes.

FC: Before I *tell* you what I have, do you mind if we take just a moment to review the parameters we *discussed?* I want to make sure that I'm on track, so I don't waste your time with something inappropriate.

Client: That's fine. Why don't we?

FC: Good. If I have it correctly, you *said* that the two of you are equal partners and that the firm's current market value is approximately $2 million. Right?

Client: That's right.

FC: You also *said* that if something happened to either of you, you both agreed that the surviving partner should be able to run the business his own way, without interference from possible heirs. Am I right?

Client: Yes.

FC: In addition, you *said* that it would take at least a year to find and train a replacement. So the surviving partner would need not only to be able to buy out the other's share from his estate, but also to replace him. Right?

Client: Yes. [The example is continued in the next section.]

Match the Features

After you review and verify the parameters of your client's need, match each parameter with the corresponding feature of your product or service. In so doing, you powerfully demonstrate the logic of your choice by showing how each feature of your product or service meets, or exceeds, the corresponding parameter of the client's problem. Remember that you are dealing with an Executive type in the auditory mode. To continue our buy-sell insurance example:

FC: You *mentioned* that you or your partner needed to be able to buy out the other's share from his estate for a million dollars. We have a policy that will not only enable you to do that more cheaply than your current plan, but will also automatically grow with your business to cover its increasing value. How does that *sound* so far?

Client: Good.

FC: You also *said* that you would need in the neighborhood of twelve months of protection while one of you sought and trained a replacement for the deceased. Your current coverage is only $400,000. It *sounds* as though you will need at least $500,000, plus additional funds to cover your lost production for the time spent searching and training. We can provide you with $750,000 worth of coverage for just a little more than you are paying now for $400,000. *Sounds* pretty good, doesn't it?

Client: Great, so far.

FC: Would you like to hear more?

Client: Yes.

At this point, your client virtually must listen to your presentation. During the profile presale, he committed to buy

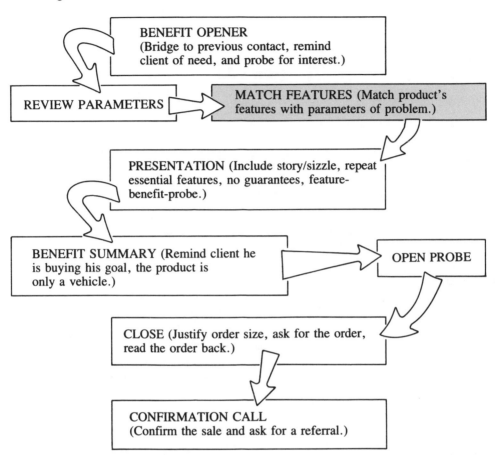

anything that matched his parameters. You have just matched or exceeded them. **When a client asks to hear more, he has already bought the product in his own mind.**

> **MATCHING YOUR PRODUCT'S FEATURES TO THE PARAMETERS OF YOUR CLIENT'S NEED IS A POWERFUL TRIAL CLOSE.**

CHAPTER 29

Putting Life into the Body of Your Sales Presentation

The opener reminds your client that he has a problem that you can solve. Reviewing the parameters starts you both at the same spot and begins the "yes set." And matching the features to the parameters begins the building of a powerful case for your product or service. The purpose of your presentation is to introduce and justify the product or service that you've selected as a solution. It leads the client through a process of understanding and identifying with your product or service as a solution to his goal. It then moves him to the close, where he formally "owns" your solution before you accept the order.

Ideally, your presentation will move the client through a series of acceptance probes that will prepare him to give you the order. To make your presentation effective, you must provide certain key data. Which information you should include will vary according to the product or service you are selling. In all cases, however, the data should be sufficiently complete to enable your client to make an *informed* decision.

You should include all the data necessary to validate your selection of the given product or service as appropriate to solve the client's problem. This is particularly important because every

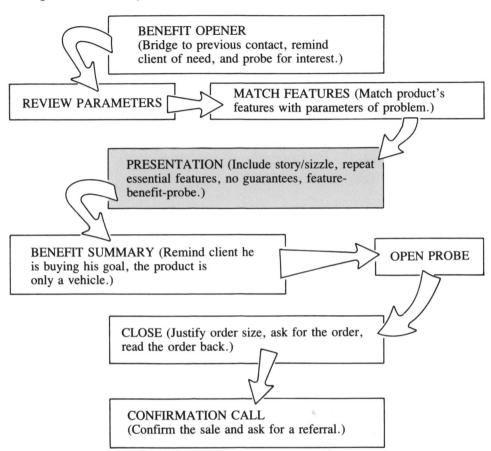

investment decision you ask a client to make involves some risk. Remember, even putting money in a vault incurs the risk of inflation.

Some clients will tell you during profiling that they want "growth," or they "just want to make money." Don't believe them! Given enough of a reason, anyone will take any risk (e.g., wouldn't you risk almost certain death to save your child?). However, without a sufficient reason, some people won't take any risk. "Making money" is an abstract concept. It may sound fine when making an investment, but it won't seem important enough to help deal with a financial loss if the investment is unsuccessful. When that happens, you, as the financial consultant, get blamed. That's why we strongly suggest that you sell the benefit (i.e., end goal of college tuition, retirement, etc.), rather than your product's or service's features (e.g., growth, income, etc.).

You can be sure that the client has enough information to make an informed decision by matching the parameters of the problem. And always give enough of a story about your product or service to provide the "sizzle" necessary to help the client emotionally identify with it.

Supporting Data

Supporting data should include, but not necessarily be limited to, the features that correspond to the parameters of the client's goal or problem. They should also include any identifying information and any negative information. It is very important to include negative data because if the client obtains that information elsewhere, he will feel cheated.

Here is a list of the kinds of data that should be included in a presentation for the securities industry:

1. **Name** of the product or service.
2. **The relative safety** of the product or service. For example, a bond's rating by S&P, or a stock's rating by your company, Moody's, Value Line, etc. (investment grade, good quality, etc.). Does this product or service fit within your client's risk tolerance for this goal?
3. **The compounded rate of expected growth of capital,** if any. For example, suppose a research report on a stock indicates an expected earnings growth of 15 percent per year. Will this growth rate enable the client to meet his goal within his required time frame?
4. **The dividend** paid, if significant or requested. For fixed-income products such as corporate bonds, include information on: **coupon, current yield, yield to maturity, and yield to call.**

5. **Call data** for fixed-income products. When and under what circumstances can a client expect to lose his ownership? When is the maturity (day-month-year)?

6. **The issuing authority,** especially for fixed-income securities.

7. The **source of funds** to pay principal and interest for fixed-income securities. Is a municipal bond **revenue** or **general obligation?** Is a corporate bond a **mortgage bond** or a **debenture?** Is it subject to the alternative minimum tax?

8. The **price** of the security or service. For bonds, be aware of the price in *yield-to-maturity basis points* as well as in dollars.

9. **A complete description** of the product or service that summarizes all features should be given before asking for the order.

The Story and the Sizzle

Sizzle has been defined as the story the client will remember after the sale. It consists of data that will enable the client to emotionally identify with the product, become excited about owning it, and believe that it will help solve his problem. In short, the story and the sizzle have three main purposes:

1. To support or justify the figures you provide when discussing your product or service's features.

2. To help your client to emotionally identify with your product or service.

3. To provide a supporting story that your client will remember *after* the sale.

EXAMPLE: To support buying Champion International stock, you tell your client that Champion is the largest owner of timberland in the world. (The company owns 6 million acres of timber, roughly equivalent to the entire state of Rhode Island and half of the state of Massachusetts.) To validate buying AT&T stock, include in your presentation the fact that AT&T is the owner of Bell Labs, the world's premier research and development facility. (Bell Labs has produced an average of one patent per day since 1906.)

Feature-Benefit-Probe

When you present the essential features of your product to your client, it is important to keep him involved in the process and to help him see the connection between his problem and your solution. To do this, you need to connect each essential fact with the problem, thereby demonstrating how that product or service fills the parameters of the problem. Then probe for acceptance.

EXAMPLE 1:

FC: Ms. Jones, this certificate of deposit is FDIC insured, providing the safety of principal to maturity that you were interested in for the down payment on that house. Don't you agree?

EXAMPLE 2:

FC: Mrs. Smith, the projected 12 percent growth of this stock should more than provide the growth that we need for your son's college fund. Wouldn't you agree?

Each of these examples connects the solution with the problem, demonstrating the logic of accepting the solution and making the suggested purchase.

Here we would like to offer a caveat regarding the sale of securities. Many of the young FCs with whom we have worked over the years have gotten caught up in the image of being a "broker." They get so excited about a given stock or bond they are selling that they actually come to believe that that particular security is vitally important (even to the customer). We believe that, with the exception of the "day trader" (who is constantly looking for the latest "hot" stock), that is not true. Here's why:

If we offered to send you on a free vacation in Florida for two weeks, all expenses paid (shows, hotel, meals, etc.), you might get excited. You would have but one problem—getting there. Obviously, you would immediately call your travel agent and tell him the parameters of your problem (destination, dates, level of comfort, speed and safety required, and how much you are willing to spend). He would then check and call back with a recommendation for your transportation. As long as his recommendation *meets, or exceeds, your parameters,* do you really care what it is? Of course not! All that you are really interested in is your destination—Florida.

The same is true of most investors. **They are interested in their end goal. As long as your recommendation meets or exceeds all of their parameters, it doesn't matter what it is!**

Buying Signals

Your client will often provide "buying signals." These may take several forms:

• Ownership questions
• Positive statements that can be built upon
• Pauses

When these signals occur, reinforce them and move to the close. (*Note:* Sometimes these signals will appear before you have completed your presentation. When this happens, reinforce them and radically shorten your presentation, but be sure to include all *essential* data. Then move to the close. Learn how to distinguish a true buying signal from a false one. This is particularly important when working with Socialites, who, because they are warm followers, they may appear to be giving a buying signal when in reality they are simply trying to obtain your approval. You should not automatically assume that your client is ready to place an order simply because you think you heard a buying signal.

EXAMPLES—OWNERSHIP QUESTIONS:

• "When will I receive the first dividend?"
• "How long until the sale settles?"
• "When will I need to transfer the funds?"

EXAMPLES: Here are some clients' positive statements that you can build upon as you close:

- "I like the safety of certificates of deposit."
- "Several of my friends own this mutual fund and they are very pleased with it."

PAUSES: Sometimes the failure to ask a question can be a buying signal. Hence silence in response to your request for questions or concerns can be very positive. Just make sure you probe to verify your interpretation of the client's silence (remember the Bureaucrat tends be silent much of the time).

> **LISTEN FOR BUYING SIGNALS.**

Benefit Summary

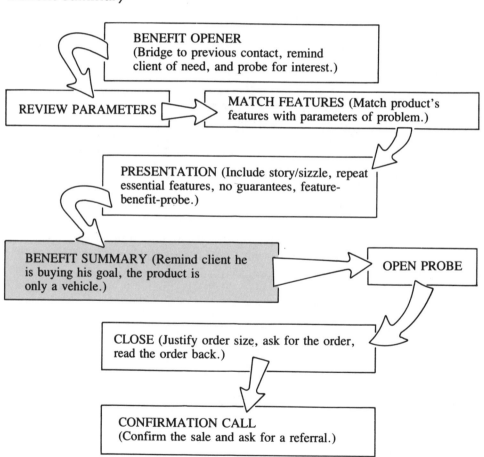

BENEFIT OPENER
(Bridge to previous contact, remind client of need, and probe for interest.)

REVIEW PARAMETERS

MATCH FEATURES (Match product's features with parameters of problem.)

PRESENTATION (Include story/sizzle, repeat essential features, no guarantees, feature-benefit-probe.)

BENEFIT SUMMARY (Remind client he is buying his goal, the product is only a vehicle.)

OPEN PROBE

CLOSE (Justify order size, ask for the order, read the order back.)

CONFIRMATION CALL
(Confirm the sale and ask for a referral.)

Before asking for the order, it is important to summarize the links between your product's features and the benefit(s) sought by your client. This provides a final reminder to the client of why he is buying the product and prepares him for the close.

EXAMPLE:

> *FC:* Mr. Jackson, with its investment-grade safety and its projected 12 percent per year growth, I'm sure that you can see why I think that XYZ stock is such an excellent vehicle to help provide for your son's college education. Wouldn't you agree?

If your presentation has been effective, the client virtually has to agree. When he does, he has effectively bought your product.

Probing

We cannot overemphasize the importance of probing for acceptance and understanding throughout your presentation. The last time you bought a car, even if you knew all there was to know about the car, you asked questions before you bought it. Why? If you're like most people, it was because you wanted to be sure that you were doing the right thing in making that particular purchase. Given the price of that car, you could not afford to be wrong. Your clients are no different. Whenever we buy something, especially a major financial purchase for ourselves or for our company, we have a psychological need to be reassured that we are making the right choice. This is particularly true when we are purchasing something like life insurance or securities, since these are intangible products.

This desire to be right, this need for reassurance, can actually become a barrier to the sale. After all, for many people, not doing anything is better than being wrong. This is particularly true of the hostile client. As you probe for acceptance and understanding, invite questions from your client. When you answer his questions, you provide the reassurance that he seeks, thereby lowering the barrier of his concern about being right. This also reassures him that you know what you are doing.

Some FCs incorporate so much information into their presentation that they don't leave anything for the client to ask. Rather than reassure the client, this may force him to either

- remain anxious (which frequently kills the sale), or
- ask a question that is sufficiently esoteric that you won't know the answer.

If you have no answer to the client's first question, it will appear that you don't know what you are doing, which will only increase his anxiety. If you know the answer to the first question or two, the client usually won't ask any others. Once he is reassured, the sale becomes much easier.

Probing is also important to avoid "buyer's remorse." Many of us speak very rapidly when we are excited. This is especially true during a presentation. Unfortunately, that can make some clients feel rushed or pressured. One way to avoid this is to tell the client that you may speak quickly when you are enthusiastic. In addition, you should always probe for concerns after you have completed your presentation.

EXAMPLE:

> *FC:* Ms. Ellington, when I get excited, I'm afraid that I may speak very quickly. Before we go on, why don't we pause for a minute to let you catch your breath and to ask any questions you may have. Is there anything that I haven't covered, or that you'd like me to go over again?

Finally, of course, it is important to make sure that your client fully understands what you are presenting. There are times when a client will buy on faith something that he doesn't fully understand. While this may initially seem good to many FCs, such a sale can cost more than it is worth. For example, a client may call later to cancel his purchase because someone else has explained to him why it was a "bad" idea. Worse, if the security or product purchased does not perform as expected, the client may sue, claiming that he did not really understand the risks.

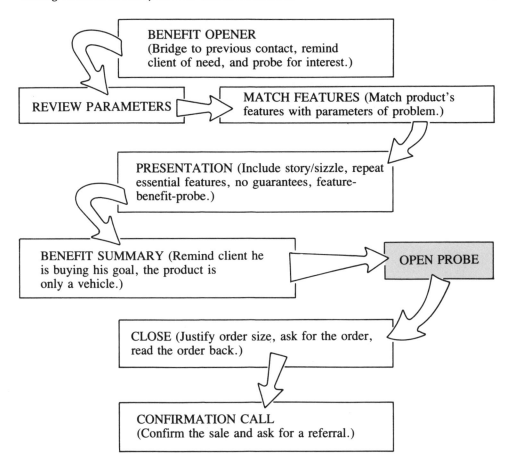

Many companies will settle with the client and make the FC pay the difference between the settlement figure and the insurance coverage for such cases.

By following the procedures that we have outlined, you will substantially increase the probability of getting the order. However, despite the best preparation in the world, you will occasionally encounter clients who "have to think it over," "have to talk it over," "have to X," before making a decision (these are typically Bureaucrat or Socialite clients, but not always). When this occurs, you need to ascertain which category their reason falls into and then respond to it. For example:

- They really do need time (e.g., they always make such decisions with their spouse).
- They need to be further motivated.
- They have another reason (e.g., they haven't got the money to invest because they spent the money they had when you profiled them).

The Close That Sells

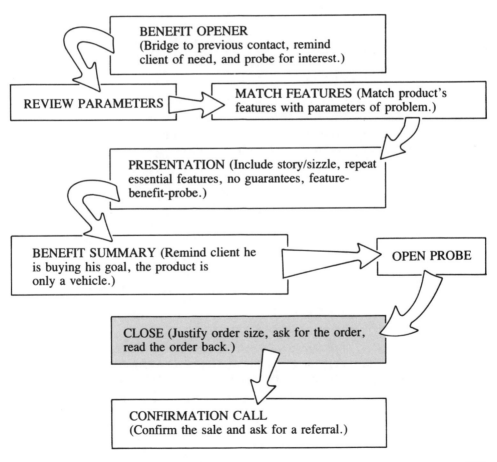

BENEFIT OPENER
(Bridge to previous contact, remind
client of need, and probe for interest.)

REVIEW PARAMETERS

MATCH FEATURES (Match product's
features with parameters of problem.)

PRESENTATION (Include story/sizzle, repeat
essential features, no guarantees, feature-
benefit-probe.)

BENEFIT SUMMARY (Remind client he
is buying his goal, the product is
only a vehicle.)

OPEN PROBE

CLOSE (Justify order size, ask for the order,
read the order back.)

CONFIRMATION CALL
(Confirm the sale and ask for a referral.)

Justifying the Order Size

Many FCs believe that you should always ask for the biggest order you can get. While sophisticated clients know how much they can spend for your product or service, as well as how much they need, it is still your responsibility to suggest an order size that is appropriate. If you don't do this, the client may feel that you don't really understand his or her needs. If you have profiled your client effectively, you already know the appropriate-size order to suggest. In addition, keep the following points in mind:

• The New York Stock Exchange has a "know your customer" rule. Failure to adequately profile your customer for appropriateness of product and size of order can result in the loss of your license to sell securities.

• Customers who are convinced to buy more than they need don't furnish repeat business and often tell their associates of their dissatisfaction.

• If you ask for "the big order" because you believe that clients customarily reveal only a small percentage of their real spendable assets, you may make a tragic error. A customer who trusts you will assume that you know what you're doing when you ask for the big order when, in reality, you have simply not properly profiled him. Why risk that hard-earned trust?

In interviews, clients have indicated that FCs who always ask for large orders seem to be reaching for their clients' wallet. They *do not* take it as a flattering sign of how important they are.

You may think the worst thing that can happen when you ask for a big order is that the order size will be reduced by the

ASKING FOR INAPPROPRIATELY LARGE ORDERS CAN
MAKE CLIENTS FEEL AS THOUGH YOU ARE MORE
INTERESTED IN YOUR COMMISSION THAN IN THEIR NEEDS.

client or that you won't get the order at all. In actuality, the worst thing may be that you *will* get the order!

EXAMPLE: A prospect/client reveals that she has $25,000 to invest. The FC, assuming that this is the tip of the iceberg, suggests that she buy 1,000 shares of XYZ stock at $25 per share, and the client agrees. Later the market corrects (goes down), and the customer sues. At the FC's trial it comes out that he put his customer's entire liquid net worth into one stock. He has demonstrated that he is neither competent, ethical, nor professional—he *did not* "know his customer."

If you have properly profiled your customer, you will know:

• His complete asset base and the funds he has available to invest in your products and services.
• His financial needs and goals.
• His risk tolerances for investments relative to those goals.

With such information, you can make order-size recommendations that are balanced and appropriate. As a result, your recommendations will not meet the kind of resistance that is generated when clients feel that you are using them.

Ideally, you will work with your clients to establish their goals and the parameters of those goals. If you do this, the order size will always be correct, and clients will find it far more difficult to turn down the order (see Section Six, "Profiling").

The simplest way to verify and justify an order size is to refer to that parameter at the beginning of the sales call.

EXAMPLE:

FC: Mr. Brown, a few minutes ago, you reiterated that you wanted to invest $25,000 toward your education goal at this time. Is that still correct? [*Unless your presentation was extremely good, or very bad, your client should stay with the parameters that you established during profiling and reiterated during the review of the parameters.*]

Asking for the Order

Any sales manager will tell you that the biggest problem with asking for the order is getting the FC to do it! The Bureaucrat (hostile follower) FC feels that there is little he can do to influence clients' behavior, and that if clients want to buy the product or service, they will ask to do so themselves. The Socialite (warm follower) FC fears that he will displease clients and that rejection may result from asking. ("If I don't ask, he may not buy. But he won't reject me.")

Both of these individuals fail to realize that while they may not be rejected for failing to ask, they will rarely get the order because most clients just won't ask to place an order themselves. Psychologically, it is easier for clients to say yes to you than to ask you to take their order.

When asking for the order, state your rationale for the size of the order, suggest that it be placed, and follow with a probe for acceptance.

EXAMPLE:

FC: Ms. Jones, when we last discussed your goal of establishing an education fund for your children, we determined to invest a total of $21,000. Based upon that and the current price of $40 per share for XYZ, I would like to suggest that we place an order for 500 shares of XYZ at the market. That will cost about $20,000 plus commission, or about $20,450 total. May I put in the order? [*While this may appear to be a long close, it justifies the size of the order to the client (she's the one who suggested $21,000; you're just telling her how many shares she can afford for that amount). It also links the order to the ultimate benefit (the children's college fund) and leads the client to the logic of placing the recommended order.*]

When determining the size of an order of securities, divide the price of the security into the amount of money available for the sale and *round down* to the nearest hundred shares. We recommend working in round lots because many clients have told us that partial lot orders (e.g., 623 shares) give them the impression that the FC is trying to get every last dollar out of them. This is certainly the last impression that you wish to create.

Once the client has accepted the order, read it back to him, and then tell him that you will call back shortly with confirmation of the sale. **Always** call back with the confirmation because

- that's what a professional does,
- it will enable you to reinforce the client's decision to buy,
- it will enable you to confirm the cost of the transaction (so the client can put the check in the mail today), and
- the confirmation call is the ideal time to ask for a referral.

EXAMPLE:

> *FC:* Ms. James, this is Ralph Johnson over at WXY Company. I'm just calling to confirm that we were able to obtain the XYZ stock at 23 7/8 per share. For 1,000 shares, that works out to $23,875 plus a commission of about $410. How does that sound?

PROFESSIONALS ALWAYS CONFIRM SALES.

CHAPTER 31

Getting Referrals

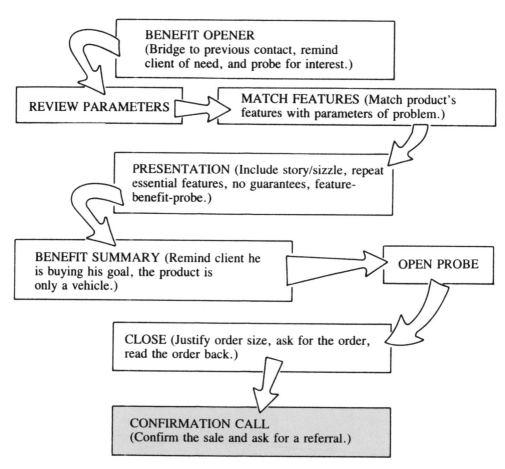

There are only three ways to increase your base of customers:

1. Beat the bushes for new customers.
2. Advertise for new customers.
3. Get referrals.

Of the three, asking for referrals is the easiest way to obtain new clients. However, as with closing a sale, the biggest problem is actually doing it. The typical reasons for a broker's procrastination are:

• Fear of rejection
• Fear of inconveniencing the client
• Forgetting or fear of being considered unprofessional

We admit that asking may result in rejection and failure to get the referral. This is especially true if you ask ineffectively. However, failing to ask for a referral almost always results in not getting one.

Some clients do feel inconvenienced when asked for a referral. Most do not feel that way at all. Many clients will feel indebted to you for helping them solve their financial problems and will be happy to have a way to repay that "debt."

Forgetting is the most common reason for not asking for a referral. We can only suggest that you find a way to remind yourself to ask until asking becomes a habit. Put a sign over your phone or include a referral question in your script.

REMEMBER REFERRALS!

A very successful FC we know did not make it a practice to ask for referrals. However, after attending a, seminar on referrals, his manager told him to try asking while he watched. The FC called a client to whom he had recently sold $800,000 in municipal bonds. When he asked her if she knew anyone else he could help, she said, "Oh my heavens! Do you accept referrals? I didn't think that you did. So, every time you sold me a bond, I told the other five girls in my bridge club, and they made the identical purchase. When they asked me if you could help them, I told them I didn't think you accepted referrals. I just told them to call your firm and open an account."

This FC was not a happy man. By failing to ask for a referral, he realized he had lost commissions on an additional $4 million in long-term municipal bond sales (that is over $80,000 in lost revenues).

Asking for the Referral

Success in asking for a referral depends on how you do it. One of the most popular methods is to ask the client if he knows anyone else who might be interested in the same type of product or service. Depending upon the type of business you do (e. g., if your clients are primarily day traders), that approach can be very effective. However, with most clients, this approach can cause several problems:

- It immediately labels you as a salesperson, thereby wiping out the impression you strove to make of being a professional financial consultant.
- Unless your client really understands your product or service, he cannot know who else needs such a purchase (until he came to you, he probably had no idea that your product was an appropriate solution to his own need).
- This approach does not utilize the client's information base of people who have similar goals or problems to solve.

Once again, think of our previous analogy of an FC being a professional just like a doctor. If you go to your doctor with a sore throat, you expect him to diagnose your problem and prescribe a solution. You do not expect him to ask you if you know anyone else who could use some penicillin. While you are not competent to diagnose or prescribe, you might know someone who is interested in finding a good doctor. Your client is no different. If he knew who needed a specific security, insurance product, and so on, he would not have had to go to you to find out that he needed it himself.

When asking for a referral, you should create the impression that giving the referral will be good for the client. Solving a problem always makes one feel good—your client may even wish to boast about it. When you ask for a referral, remember that what you are doing, in effect, is saying, "Ms. Jones, do you know someone to whom I can make you look good by helping them the way I have you?" For example:

> *FC:* Ms. Jones, I think we've done a good job of taking care of the kids' college education today. Wouldn't you agree? (*If she agrees, she has just admitted that you have done her a service and she "owes" you one in return.*]
>
> *Mrs. Jones:* Yes.
>
> *FC:* Can you think of anyone else with college-bound children whom I might be able to help the same way? [*While she might not be able to determine who needs XYZ stock, she certainly knows people who have children they are planning on sending to college.*]

Our experience shows that asking clients specifically for the names of family or friends can be threatening because it is perceived as intrusive. But if the FC describes the kinds of problems to be solved (such as affording college or saving for retirement), the request for referrals becomes less threatening and still triggers associations that will make it easy for the client to remember names. This is because we sort people in our memories by the things we share in common with them.

> EXAMPLE: If you ask me who needs a good stockbroker, I have no idea. But if you ask me who has children to send to college; or who is concerned about saving for their retirement; or even who would like to save up to buy a sixty-foot, two-masted

sloop, I can give you many names—and a stockbroker could help each of them. These questions relate to goals or problems that I am concerned about. I've discussed them with friends, family, and associates with similar concerns. Hence I can easily recall the names of those who share these goals with me.

The "Yes Set"

Throughout our discussion of the sales track, we have referred to the "yes set." As explained in Chapter 28, a "yes set" is a mental set that you establish within your client as you lead him through the sales track. You accomplish this by probing for assent with leading questions that are based upon needs (benefits) the client has already stated. Once established, the "yes set" is very helpful in reducing or actually eliminating sales resistance. It does this by helping the client perceive the logic of the solution you've chosen for his goal or problem. In addition, each time the client assents to something you've said, he psychologically "leans" toward you and finds it increasingly difficult to say "no."

It is very important that the questions you use be relevant to the presentation and the client's needs, rather than conversational queries. For example, when making a sale of stock, you could follow this script:

OPENING   *FC:* Mr. Jones, this is John Doe at Merrill Lynch. The last time we spoke, you indicated that your chief concern was establishing a college fund for the children. Is that still your primary goal?

Client: Yes.

FC: I believe I have a solution to your problem. Do you have a minute?

Client: Yes.

*REVIEW PARAM-
ETERS*

FC: Before we begin, would you mind if we reviewed the parameters that we selected when we discussed your invest- ment goals? I want to make sure that I'm still on track with what you want.

Client: That's fine.

FC: Good. When we discussed the problem, we determined that the solution would have to provide the safety of at least a good-quality investment, and would have to grow at a com- pounded rate of at least 10 percent a year. Isn't that right?

Client: Yes.

FC: And finally, that you wanted to invest $20,000 in this solution at this time. Is that still the case?

Client: Yes.

*MATCH
FEATURES TO
PARAMETERS*

FC: The solution I have in mind is rated as good quality by Merrill Lynch and Standard and Poor's. In addition, our anal- ysts expect its value to grow by at least 12 percent per year for the next five years. Would you like to hear more?

Client: Yes.

PRESENTATION

FC: What I have found for you is the common stock of XYZ Communications. You're familiar with the company, aren't you?

Client: Yes.

FC: What you may not know is that XYZ is rated as a good- quality stock. In addition, Merrill's analysts believe that their earnings per share will grow at a rate of 12 percent a year for the next five years. If the market continues to value the stock as it has in the past, we should see the price appreciate similarly. Doesn't that sound within the parameters we set?

Client: Yes.

[Sizzle.]

FC: And you know that XYZ will be around for a long time. Did you know that prior to the breakup, XYZ had to license its patents to anyone who wanted them because XYZ was a mo- nopoly?

Client: No.

FC: Now that they are no longer a monopoly, every one of their patents will start making money for them. Bluebell Labs, which is owned by XYZ, is considered the premier research and development facility in the world. I don't know if you are aware of this, but they have produced an average of one patent every day since 1906! Isn't that amazing?

Client: Yes.

FC: In addition, with the work that XYZ is doing on computers, especially the supercomputer and computer networking, our analysts consider XYZ to be ABC's only significant competitor in the next decade. When you combine that with XYZ's lead in the international communications competition, I'm sure that you can see why I feel it is such a good choice for the college fund. Right?

Client: Right.

FC: Last but not least, XYZ pays a significant dividend of 5.4 percent and has not missed a dividend payment in over seventy-five years. How does that sound?

Client: Great.

BENEFIT SUM-
MARY

FC: That is great! I'm glad you are as excited about XYZ as I am. I'm sure you can see from the expected growth, the relative safety, and the dividend why I'm recommending XYZ for the children's college fund.

Client: Yes, I can.

PROBE FOR CON-
CERNS/
UNDERSTAND-
ING

FC: Do you have any questions at this time?

Client: Yes. Did you say that XYZ hasn't missed a dividend payment in over seventy-five years?

FC: Yes. Isn't that the kind of dependability you are looking for in an investment for the children's college fund?

Client: Yes.

FC: Great! Do you have any other questions? Anything at all?

Client: No.

CLOSE
[Verify order size.]

FC: Now, when we reviewed the parameters for the college fund a moment ago, you indicated that you wanted to invest a total of $20,000 at this time. Is that still your wish?

Client: Yes.

[Ask for the order.]

FC: Good. Based upon a current market price of $24.50 per

share, I would like to suggest that we place an order for 800 shares, at the market. May I place the order?

Client: Yes.

[Read the order back.]

FC: That's great, Mr. Jones. Let me read the order back to you. We are going to place an order for 800 shares of XYZ at the market. Right?

Client: Right.

FC: Fine. I'll put in the order and call back shortly with a confirmation. Mr. Jones, I think you've made a great decision in buying XYZ for the children's education. Thanks very much. I'll call back shortly. Good-bye.

Client: Good-bye.

Did you notice how the client was moved from one assent to another until he reached the point where the FC asked for the order? Throughout the sales presentation, the client was constantly reminded that everything that occurred was really his idea and was being accomplished at his wish. As a result, it became very difficult for him to disagree with himself.

WHEN THE FC WORKS FROM THE CLIENT'S POINT OF VIEW, REFUSAL TO ACCEPT AN ORDER IS MORE THAN ILLOGICAL, IT IS IRRATIONAL.

After receiving the confirmation, the FC calls the client and asks for a referral.

[Confirm the order and ask for the referral.]

FC: Mr. Jones, John Doe here at Merrill Lynch. I called back to tell you that we got you 800 shares of XYZ at $24.50 per share. I want to tell you again that I think we've made a good start at funding the children's college education. Before I go, can you think of anyone else who might have children going to college, be retiring, or be interested in lowering their taxes whom I might be able to help?

Client: Yes. Their names are . . .

Needless to say, it is very important that your *primary* interest be to help the client and not to make a commission for yourself. Used by someone who does not put his client's interest first, the "yes set" can be very manipulative.

CHAPTER 33

Sales Scripts

The following is an example of a generic sales script. It follows the format provided in the text.

BENEFIT OPENER

---

*[If the answer is "Yes," continue. If "no," set up an appointment to call back. Remember to couch the script in **visual, auditory,** or **kinesthetic** predicates, based upon your profile of this client.]*

FC: Mr. (*client's name*), this is (*your name*), calling from (*your firm*). Do you have a moment to talk?

[Give benefit and use the client's **Buying Motivations;** *remember to respond to the psychological profile—*Executive, Socialite, Bureaucrat, *or* Dictator—*the client is currently demonstrating].*

FC: That's great. The last time we spoke, you indicated that your primary interest was in (*benefit*). Is that still the case? Good. I think I may have a solution for you. Would you like to hear about it?

Client: Yes.

REVIEW PARAMETERS

FC: Great! Before we begin, would you mind if we took just a moment to review the parameters we established when we met? I want to make sure that I'm still on track with you and that we make the best use of your time.

Client: Go ahead.

FC: You said that you needed (*list the previously agreed-upon parameters here*). Is that still the case?

Client: Yes.

MATCH PRODUCT OR SERVICE FEATURES TO THE PARAMETERS

[Compare each feature to its appropriate parameter—this demonstrates, by matching or exceeding each parameter, why you selected this solution. It is particularly important to utilize the client's **buying motivations** *here.]*

FC: Good. The solution that I've found for you has the following features: (*List features.*) Would you like to hear more?

Client: Yes.

PRESENTATION

*[Give the **story/
sizzle** of your
product/service
(use the client's
buying motivations
and **psychological
profile**), repeating
the important
features (use the
**feature–benefit–
probe technique**)
and demonstrating
how your story sup-
ports those
features].*

FC: Mr. (*client's name*), one of the reasons that I like this particular solution is: _____.

BENEFIT SUMMARY

*[Match several
FEATURES to his
BENEFIT.]*

FC: I'm sure that you can see from the (*features*) why I think that (*your product/service*) is such an excellent vehicle for helping you to attain your goal of (*benefit*). Wouldn't you agree?

Client: Yes.

OPEN PROBE

FC: Before we continue, why don't we pause for a moment to give you a chance to catch your breath. Do you have any questions about what I've covered? For that matter, is there anything you'd like to know that I haven't covered, or that you'd like me to go over again?

*[CLAP and respond
to his question.
Then probe to see if
he has any more
questions. Continue
this until he has no
more questions.]*

Client: I do have one question. What . . . ?

CLOSE

[*Justify the order size.*]   *FC:* A moment ago you reiterated your desire to spend (*insert dollar parameter or number of units desired*). Is that still the case?

Client: Yes.

[*Ask for the order.*]   *FC:* In that case, I would suggest that we place an order for (*amount*). May I put in the order?

Client: Yes.

[*Read the order back to the customer.*]   *FC:* Great! That's (*number of units*), at (*$ each*). I'll place the order and call you back with a confirmation of the sale. Thank you very much. Good-bye.

(*Note:* Remember, when you call back with the confirmation, always ask for a referral.)

Self-Evaluation

As with prospecting calls, it is useful to periodically tape-record a sales call and listen to it for your strengths and weaknesses. In Appendix 6 (see page 300), we have provided examples of self-evaluation forms for both prospecting and sales calls. Make it a habit to evaluate the quality of your calls at least twice a week.

Position Building

Many FCs spend a great deal of time trying to follow twenty, thirty, or even forty different stocks at a time. Frequently they do this because they are looking for the next great performer—the stock that will make them look like a hero to their clients. It's important to remember that most clients want their money to grow consistently over a long period of time. Those who do look for the "quick kill" are gamblers who usually lose more than they gain and then blame it on their broker.

For this reason, we suggest that you select no more than twelve stocks to follow at any one time. Use them to solve the problems of all your clients who have parameters that match the stocks' features. Generally, you will want four or five solid, investment-grade equities from varied industries, three or four good-quality equities, and two or three speculative equities. It is also useful to include two or three utilities or other income-producing equities among those you follow and recommend.

To effectively build a position in a stock or other product, review your clients' profile sheets until you find someone who has a goal or problem and whose parameters would be met, or exceeded, by the features of the stock. Then copy the account information and the parameters from the profile. Continue through your profile sheets until you have a list of clients for whom this stock would be a good solution. When you have completed your list, write a script for your stock or product, leaving blanks for the clients' parameters and the product's story/sizzle and features.

Exhibit 33-1 is an example of a position-building worksheet for selling XYZ stock at $32 per share. It is investment-grade (IG) quality and expected to grow at an annual rate of 14% per year for the next five years.

Cross Posting

It is a good idea to "cross-post" your holdings. To do this, keep a separate sheet for each product that you sell and list every customer that owns that product on the sheet. This is extremely useful for three reasons:

1. Many firms require it to meet compliance regulations.
2. It provides you with a list of whom to call if the product's value goes up or down,
3. It provides you with a list of owners of the product who will be interested in updates on general information about the product and its expected performance in the future.

Generally, you should maintain the following information about each customer on the sheet:

EXHIBIT 33-1
Position-Building Worksheet

| Product: XYZ | | | | | Parameters | | | |
Name	Phone #	Account #	Benefit	$	#Shrs.	Risk	% growth
John Doe	654-3210	12-4576	Kids' college	$20K	600	GQ	12%/yr.
Sally Jones	987-6543	12-7693	Retirement	$30K	900	IG	12%/yr.
Bill Smith	123-4567	12-3357	Vac. home	$10K	300	GQ	14%/yr.
Etc.							

- Name.
- Telephone number.
- Account number.
- Amounts of the product (e.g., number of shares) that the client owns.
- Why the client bought the product (the desired benefit; e.g., children's college fund).
- When the client bought each block of the product.
- The price the client paid for each block.

The form (Exhibit 33-2) will look similar to the one used for position building.

After the Sale

After you have confirmed the sale to the client, reinforce his decision by sending him additional information on the product. If it is a stock, send a copy of the latest year-end report (the company will be happy to send you a box of these), your firm's opinion on the company, and (if you have an agreement with Standard and Poor's or Moody's) rating companies' opinions. Doing this reinforces your selection of the product as a solid answer to the client's need by demonstrating that several experts all agreed the product or stock was a good choice.

EXHIBIT 33-2
Cross Posting

Product: _____						
Name	*Phone #*	*Account #*	*Amount*	*Benefit*	*Dates*	*Price*

When you review the financial news each morning, scan for information relating to the companies or industries that you follow. When you find something, consult your cross-posting sheet on the product or company and send copies to everyone who owns it. If it's neutral or good news, send it without comment. If the news is moderately negative, send it with an explanation of why your firm still likes the product. Doing this accomplishes four things:

1. It shows your professionalism.
2. It enables you to maintain positive contact with all your clients at least monthly, without taking much time.
3. It prevents your customer from thinking that you have concealed bad news if he hears it somewhere else first.
4. It avoids having clients think that you only contact them when you want to sell them something.

Remember, your professionalism is the single most important thing that you communicate through both words and actions.

A PROFESSIONAL ALWAYS PUTS THE CLIENT FIRST!

Making a Sale: From Cold Call to Close

The following script is an example of a dialogue between a financial consultant and a client from the opening of the first prospecting call to the confirmation call following a sale.

Cold Call

[Generic opener, using unspecified sensory-oriented words.]

FC: How are you, Doctor? My name is John Doe and I'm calling from XYZ Company with some information on the latest changes in the tax laws. Are you familiar with us?

[Visual orientation.]

Client: Yes. I've *seen* your advertisements on television.

FC: That's great. Are you familiar with the latest changes in the tax code and the impact that they will have upon your investments?

[Resistance. More visual words.]

Client: I think that my current broker at ABC Company is *looking after* my affairs quite well, thank you.

[Responds using visual words. Attempts to overcome the resistance.]

FC: That's great! It's nice to run into someone who is being well taken care of in the current market. *Look,* my firm is taking an informal poll. Would you mind if I asked you one question before I go?

Client: What?

[Continues to respond using visual words.]

FC: The last time you *saw* your broker for a quarterly *review* of your investment plan, did he *show* you the latest changes in the tax codes and *outline* their effects upon your investments?

Client: No, he didn't.

[Continues to match the prospect's visual words.]

FC: Dr. Jones, we've put together an information series to enable investors to *examine* the latest tax changes and get a *clearer picture* of their effects. Would you like me to send it to you?

Client: All right.

[Gives rationale for asking questions.]
[Continues to use visual words.]

FC: That's fine. I'll put the information in the mail today. So that I don't waste your time sending you hundreds of pages that don't really apply to your situation, would you mind if I asked you a few questions to help *pinpoint* your tax concerns?

Client: What kind of questions?

FC: Well, for example, what is your greatest tax concern at this time?

Client: What do you mean?

[Visual words, nonthreatening qualifying questions.]

FC: For example, do you expect to *see* a large passive income this year? Or is your tax bracket too high? Are you subject to the alternative minimum tax? Questions like that. Is that all right?

Client: OK.

[Visual words.]

FC: All right, let's *take a look* at your needs. Are you subject to the alternative minimum tax?

[From his passive resistance, this prospect may be a Bureaucrat.]

Client: I don't know. What is it?

[Visual words.]

FC: The alternative minimum tax was established to make sure that those who have too many tax-advantaged investments still pay some taxes. It works out to 20 percent of your investments, and can be a real shock when you *see* a *notice* of an IRS audit. Why don't we *examine* a few more areas to *see* if you are subject or not. All right?

Client: OK.

FC: Is tax on your income a significant problem at this time?

Client: Yes. I'm in the highest bracket and the IRS has eliminated my deductions for dependents.

[*Open probe using visual words to draw out possible Bureaucrat prospect.*]

FC: That *looks* like a real problem. My I ask what steps you've already taken to deal with this?

[*Visual words.*]

Client: Why?

[*This prospect is probably qualified: He has a broker; he's in the highest tax bracket; and he owns municipal bonds.*]

FC: Well, among other things, the types of steps you've taken may help *clarify* whether or not you're subject to the additional alternate minimum tax we're *examining.*

Client: All right. I have a lot of municipal bonds that give me a tax-free income.

FC: That's great. Do you know whether or not they are private purpose bonds?

Client: No. What are private-purpose bonds?

[*Visual word.*]

FC: Well, some bonds can actually cause problems with the alternative minimum tax. We may want to sit down and *look* at them in detail, later. Can you give me an idea of what other types of investments you have?

Client: I don't know whether I should.

[*CLAPs, using visual word to show that he understands.*]

FC: Dr. Jones, it *appears* as though you are still a little uncomfortable answering these questions for a stranger over the telephone. Is that right?

[*Visual word.*]

Client: Yes. I've never *seen* you before, and I don't know you.

[*Continues to CLAP using visual word.*]

FC: I can understand that. I don't know how comfortable I'd be answering questions for someone I'd never *seen* either. May I make a suggestion?

Client: Sure. What?

[*Continues matching the prospect's visual words.*]
[*Introduces the idea of a later meeting.*]

FC: I'll send you something to *read* on the alternative minimum tax that will help you *get a clearer picture* of it. Then, why don't we make an appointment for you to come into my office later in the week to go over this *in person* and you can *see* how I work? Then, when you're feeling more comfortable, we can *look at* your investments together *to see* how the tax changes will affect them. How does that *look* to you?

[*Visual words.*]

Client: OK. That *looks* good to me. Send me the material and I'll *examine it.*

[*Visual word.*]

FC: Great! I'll send it out today and you should receive it by Thursday. Why don't I call you on Friday to *see* if you have any questions? When is a good time to reach you?

Client: Fine. Call me after three.

[*Sets up business appointment to call back. Uses visual word.*]
[*Repeats his name and the company's.*]

FC: All right. Dr. Jones, I'll send the materials today, and I will call you at three thirty on Friday to *see* if you have any questions on the alternative minimum tax. Again, my name is John Doe from XYZ, and I'll call at three thirty. Thank you very much. Good-bye.

Client: Good-bye.

Friday Callback

[*Uses bridging opener and visual words.*]

FC: Dr. Jones? This is John Doe over at XYZ Company. When we spoke on Tuesday, I promised to call back to *see* if you had any questions on the alternative minimum tax. How does it *look?*

[*Visual word.*]

Client: Frankly, I'm not sure. It's not really very *clear,* even with your materials.

[*Matches the prospect's visual/sensory orientation.*]

FC: I can *see* how that might be pretty frustrating. Is that how it *looks* to you?

Client: Yes.

[*Sets up face-to-face meeting. Continues using visual words.*]

FC: Then may I suggest that we meet and *look at it* together. Maybe that way I can help you *get a better perspective.*

Client: All right. When?

FC: How would Monday at five thirty be?

Client: That would be fine.

[*Verifies that the prospect knows the address.*]

FC: That's great! Do you have our address?

Client: You're right across from the bank on the corner of Fourth Street and Jacob Lane, aren't you?

[*Visual words.*]

FC: That's right. I'll *see* you at five thirty on Monday in my office. Thank you very much. *See* you on Monday.

Client: Good-bye.

Monday Face-to-Face Meeting

[*Visual word.*]

FC: Dr. Jones? John Doe. How are you? It's so nice to *see* you. Won't you sit down?

[*Visual word.*]

Client: Thank you. You have a nice office. It's very *attractive.*

[Matches visual word.]

FC: Thank you. Have you had a chance to give the alternative minimum tax a second *look?*

[Visual words.]

Client: Yes. But I'm still not sure whether or not it applies to me. Sometimes my investments seem so complicated that it's hard to get a *clear picture* of them.

[Acknowledges the prospect's comments by using same visual orientation.]

FC: It is pretty complicated, isn't it? May I make a suggestion? Why don't we take a few minutes and *review* your situation and *see* if we can't put it all into some kind of *perspective.*

Client: OK.

[Sets up profiling.] [Gives rationale and obtains permission to take notes.]

FC: What I'd like to do is to build a profile of your investment goals and the steps that you've already taken to obtain them. Because I want to be certain to remember everything, and because I'm going to give you a copy when I'm through, I'm going to take notes while we speak. Is that all right?

Client: Certainly.

[Visual word.]

FC: Good. Can you give me a *picture* of your investment goals?

Client: Sure. I want to make money and lower my taxes.

[Uses visual word; probes for underlying goal.]

FC: That makes sense. Dr. Jones, at the risk of *appearing* a little silly, I need to ask you what you want to make the money for.

Client: Why?

[Explains the importance of risk and the underlying goal.]

FC: Because every investment decision involves some degree of risk. Even not making a decision and keeping all of your money in cash would involve the risk of inflation. Most of us have different levels of tolerance for risks, depending upon the purpose of the investment. For example, some people wish their retirement investments to be virtually risk free, but are willing to accept some risk in their investments to gain greater growth for a vacation home. Usually, the greater the growth potential, the greater the risk.

Client: I want to make money to secure my retirement.

[Explores goals.]

FC: That's great. Do you have any other goals—the children's education, perhaps.

Client: Yes, that's certainly important.

FC: Any others? A second home or a boat or a plane?

Client: No. That's it.

[Visual word.]

FC: Ok then, it *looks* like we have three investment goals: to lower your taxes, secure your retirement, and pay for your children's education. Now let's prioritize them. Which is the most important and which the least?

[Uses visual word; gives priorities.]

Client: Let's see . . . I guess the children's education is the most important, and lowering the taxes is actually the least.

[Verifies priorities.]

FC: So, it would *appear* that the order of priority is, first, children's education; second, retirement; and third, lowering your taxes. Is that right?

Client: Yes.

[Visual word.]

FC: Ok. Now let's take a moment to *explore* each in detail. How many children do you have?

Client: Two. One is ten and the other, five.

[Uses visual word; explores costs.]

FC: So we have eight years and thirteen years, respectively, before they go to college. Have you *pinpointed* what kind of school you wish them to attend and what the costs will be when each of them begins?

Client: Frankly, I just assumed that they would attend my alma mater, Harvard.

[Visual word.]
[Explores costs.]
[Assumes that they will be working to-gether.]

FC: All right. Harvard *seems* to be around $13,000 per year right now, just for tuition. With room, board, and expenses, you would need close to $20,000 per year per child today. College costs have been rising at a rate of nearly 8 percent per year. At that rate, they will double every nine years. That means that when your oldest child reaches college age, the costs will be about $40,000 per year. For your youngest, the cost will be closer to $55,000. That means that we'll need about $160,000 for your eldest, and $220,000 for your youngest. Have you considered these kinds of figures before?

[Visual word.]

Client: They are very high. But they are not totally unexpected. When I *saw* the alumni director, he warned me what the costs might be.

[Elicits current holdings.]

FC: Can you tell me what steps you've already taken in *regard* to paying for your children's schooling?

Client: I established education funds for each child when they were born. Each currently holds about $60,000 in certificates of deposit that we roll over every six months.

[Visual words.]

FC: That *looks* pretty good. Can you give me a *picture* of when the CDs will be due to roll over again?

Client: In about five weeks.

FC: Fine. How often do you add money to the children's accounts?

Client: We don't have a regular schedule. We were going to put some more in this year.

[Educates the prospect.]
[Visual word.]

FC: The reason I ask is that if you put in enough to pay the costs of tuition this year, you only need to stay ahead of inflation and taxes to have enough when they attend. You *recognize* that you have to pay taxes on the interest from those CDs each year until the children reach fourteen? Then they pay the taxes at their lower rate.

[Visual words.]

Client: Yes. My accountant told us and you can *plainly see* that we're not very happy about it. That's one of the reasons that we're concerned about taxes.

FC: Can you put an additional $20,000 into each child's account this year?

Client: Yes, we can do that.

[Visual word.]
[Verifies risk tolerance.]

FC: Good. Then all we'll need to do is keep ahead of tuition inflation and you won't have to worry about their education anymore. I do need to ask what level of safety you desire. It *looks,* from your having bought CDs, like you want maximum safety. Is that right?

Client: Yes. I want the children's education funds to be virtually risk free.

FC: What return are you getting on the CDs in the children's accounts?

Client: About 6 percent.

[Educates prospect about need for greater return.]
[Visual word.]
[Visual word; commits prospect to change.]

FC: That's pretty good. Unfortunately, after deducting for your taxes, that leaves only 4 percent growth. And that's only about half the annual rate of increase in tuition. Right now, it *looks* as though you'll need to either keep putting money into their accounts each year or change to an investment that can keep you ahead of inflation and taxes. If I could *show* you an investment that provides the safety you require and a higher rate of return, would you consider switching?

Client: Certainly.

[Reviews parameters for commitment.]

FC: There are several possibilities. Let me just review these parameters. You need maximum safety, growth after taxes of at least 8 percent per year for the next eight to thirteen years, and you want to invest $80,000 per child. Is that right?

[Prospect uncon-sciously commits himself to buy any-thing meeting these parameters.]	*Client:* Yes. *FC:* Good. Now, if I understood you clearly, your next priority is retirement. Is that right? *Client:* Yes.
[Elicits parame-ters.]	*FC:* When are you planning to retire? *Client:* If possible, when I'm fifty-five, in twenty years.
[Visual word.]	*FC: Looks* good to me. What kind of income will you want to see, in today's dollars? Remember, your expenses after retire-ment are usually only one-half to two-thirds of what they are when you are working. *Client:* The house will be paid for then, and so will the kids' schooling. I think $60,000 a year would do it.
[Visual words.]	*FC:* Ok. Can you *paint me a picture* of what you've already done for retirement? *Client:* I have a Keogh Plan. Each year I've funded it with the maximum amount. Right now, I have about $200,000 in it. *FC:* That's certainly a good start. Other than Social Security, is there anything else? An IRA, perhaps? *Client:* Yes. My wife and I each have IRAs. I think there's about $12,000 in each.
[Visual words.] *[Buying motivation.]*	*FC:* Ok. Can you *give me a picture* of what kinds of investments you have in your Keogh and IRA accounts? *Client:* The IRAs just have short-term CDs that roll over auto-matically. The Keogh has half in a *high-quality* mutual fund and half in a jumbo CD that rolls over. It comes due again next month with all of the others.
[Elicits risk tol-erance.] *[Visual word.]*	*FC:* That's fine. Dr. Jones, if you had invested $100,000 in your Keogh six months ago, and received a call today saying that you had lost money, how much could you walk away from before you *saw* red?
[Visual word.]	*Client:* I'd be upset if any of it were lost. I don't like taking risks with my money. That's why most of it is in bank CDs—especially the way the stock market *looks*.
[Visual words.] *[Verifies data.]*	*FC:* All right, Doctor, I'll put this through the computer tonight, and tomorrow I'll be able to give you a *clear perspective* on how much money you'll need to have at retirement to provide the kind of income you want. Let's *review* what you've told me: You currently have $200,000, evenly divided between a jumbo

CD and a mutual fund, in your Keogh account. And you have another $24,000 in IRAs for your wife and yourself, in short-term CDs. What kind of mutual fund?

[Visual word.]

Client: It's the MNO High-Quality Total Return Fund. My broker suggested it as a way of *seeing* us through inflation while providing income that is automatically reinvested.

[Elicits buying motivation.]

FC: That makes sense. Is that what you like about it, growth and reinvestable income?

[Buying motivations.]
[Visual word.]

Client: Not really. I like its *safety* and *convenience*. The income is reinvested automatically and I don't have to waste time *looking* after it.

[Verifies consistency of safety and convenience as key criteria for investing. These are consistent for a Bureaucrat.]

FC: Would that be the same with the short-term CDs? Safety and rolling over automatically?

Client: Yes. I don't want to have to spend a *great deal of time* being bothered about my investments. I just want something that is safe and convenient to use that's not too difficult to understand.

[Visual words.]

FC: That seems *pretty clear* to me. Would you like me to *look* into our research regarding the fund's performance and let you know our *view* of it?

Client: Thank you. That would be fine.

[Visual word.]

FC: Now, last but not least, your taxes. You mentioned that you have several municipal bonds. Can you give me an *angle* on the type and number of bonds that you have?

Client: Yes. I have twelve different bonds to provide diversity. Each is worth $25,000. I think they're paying about 5 percent, but last year I had to pay taxes on part of them. Is that the alternative minimum tax you talked about?

FC: It may be. Do you do your own tax returns or do you have an accountant?

Client: I use an accountant.

[Visual words.]

FC: That's good. If you'd like, I could *see* him and the three of us could *look* at this together.

Client: That would be great.

[Visual word.]
[Educates the prospect.]

FC: At the moment, it *appears* as though you have sacrificed price and efficiency to obtain diversification. If your bonds are insured, three different bonds of $100,000 each would give you a better price and be just as safe or safer than twelve little bonds.

Client: Really? I didn't know that.

[Visual word.]

FC: Why don't we make an appointment to *see* your accountant? Then the three of us can develop an investment plan that is consistent with your needs.

Client: All right. I'll call him now. Can I use your phone?

[Prospect calls and sets up joint appointment.]

FC: Certainly.

[Visual word.]
[See Exhibit 34-1.]

FC: Doctor, why don't I make you a *copy* of these notes I've taken? Then when we meet with your accountant on Tuesday, we'll be starting at the same place.

Client: Thank you.

[Uses visual words; presells tomorrow's recommendation.]

FC: Here's your copy. Let's *review* it briefly now, to make sure that the information I have is correct. Tonight I'll *see* what kinds of investments fit the criteria we established for the children's education. Then tomorrow, I'll call you with a *clear-cut* idea. What do you think?

Client: Great. *See* you then. Good-bye.

Sales Call

[Verifies that his client has time to talk now.]

FC: Hello, Doctor. This is John Doe at XYZ. Do you have a moment?

Client: Certainly.

[Benefit opener; uses visual word.]

FC: When I *saw* you yesterday, you indicated that your primary concern was your children's education. Is that right?

[Begins "yes set."]

Client: Yes.

[Visual word.]

FC: I think that I may have found a solution for you that is as painless as possible. Would you like me to *sketch* it out for you?

Client: Sure. Go ahead.

EXHIBIT 34-1
Profile Sheet

Buying Criteria:
 Safety, convenience
 Does not like stock
  market.

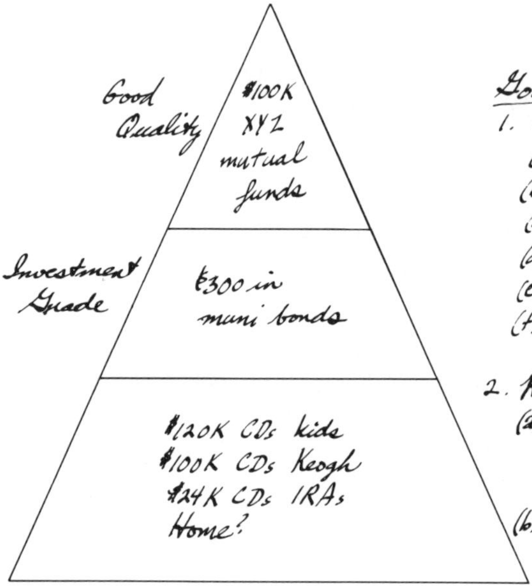

Dr. Richard Jones
1 Somewhere Dr.
Anywhere, U.S. 21095
Phone: 765-4321

Good Quality — $100K XYZ mutual funds

Investment Grade — $300 in muni bonds

$120K CDs kids
$100K CDs Keogh
$24K CDs IRAs
Home?

Goals:
1. Children's education:
   (a) $60K/child – short-term CDs
   (b) NO risk
   (c) Growth ≥ 8%/yr.
   (d) #1 child – Mary – 10 y.o. (8 yrs)
   (e) #2 child – Adam – 5 y.o. (13 yrs.)
   (f) $20K each child to invest now.

2. Retirement:
   (a) Keogh – $200K ($100K in jumbo CD, $100K in mutual fund).
   (b) 2 IRAs – $12K each in short-term CDs

3. Taxes:
   12 different muni bonds
   ($25K each: average yield = 5%)

Note: Meet w/ accountant and Dr. Jones, Tuesday, to review alternative minimum tax and his retirement funds.

Personal:
 Married: wife Edna
 2 children
   Mary 10 y.o.
   Adam 5 y.o.
 Age 46

Insurance?
Home?
Wife work?
Additional assets?
   Investments?
Liabilities?

[Visual word; reviews parameters.]	*FC:* Great. *Look,* before we begin, I'd like to *review* our parameters once more to make sure that I'm still on track. Is that all right?
[Continue "yes set."]	*Client:* OK.
	FC: All right. You said that you wanted something that was absolutely safe. Right?
	Client: Yes.
	FC: And it will have to grow, after taxes, faster than the 8 percent tuition increases that colleges are expected to make. Right?
	Client: Right.
[Visual words.]	*FC:* Finally, you indicated that you wanted to invest $20,000 in each of the children's accounts now, with the rest being added when the CDs mature. Have I *got the picture?*
	Client: Yes.
[Match features.] *[Visual words.]*	*FC:* Great! The investment that I have for you is fully insured and is backed by the taxing power of the state of Pennsylvania. How does that *look* for safe?
	Client: Great so far.
[Visual word.]	*FC:* Next, it has a compound rate of return of 8½ percent from now until your daughter graduates in eight years, and a rate of 9 percent until your son graduates in thirteen years. Isn't that an *eyeful?*
	Client: Yes. But I thought we needed those rates after taxes.
[Matches buying motivations.] *[Visual word.]*	*FC:* They *are* after taxes. And another nice feature is that you don't have to worry about the inconvenience of reinvesting the income. Would you like to *see* more?
	Client: Absolutely!
[Presentation.] *[Visual word.]*	*FC:* What I've found for you is a zero coupon Pennsylvania municipal bond. Because it is a zero coupon bond, it pays no interest until maturity. It just compounds on itself until it reaches its full face value on its maturity date, two months before each child begins college. *Looks* good, doesn't it?
	Client: Yes, it does.
[Compares product with competition.] *[Visual word.]*	*FC:* In addition, it's insured by the Municipal Bond Insurance Agency against default of either principal or interest. And that's

for the full amount, too. Not like the bank CDs, which are only insured to the first $100,000. Add the insurance of the taxing power of the state (Pennsylvania ran a surplus last year), and I think that you can *see* just how safe this bond is. Wouldn't you agree?

Client: Yes.

[Presents and re-peats the essential features.]

FC: The actual bonds that I've selected are identical except for their maturity dates. One for each child. They are the zero coupon, MBIA-insured, Pennsylvania general obligation bonds with yields to maturity of 8½ percent and 9 percent, respectively. They cannot be called early by the state, and the price is very reasonable.

Client: What is the price?

[Visual word.]
[Benefit summary; uses visual word.]

FC: For your eldest, the price is $497.50 per bond. With $20,000, we can buy $40,000 face value. *Looks* good, doesn't it? And for your youngest, the price is $347.68 per $1,000 of face value. So, for $20,000, we can buy $57,000 of face value. I'm sure you can *see,* from the safety, the convenience, and the return, why I think that these bonds *look* like such an excellent investment for your children's Harvard education. Wouldn't you agree?

Client: Yes.

[Opens probe to forestall "buyer's remorse."]

FC: Great. Before we go any further, I know that I speak awfully quickly when I'm excited. Why don't we take a moment to catch our breath and give you a chance to ask any questions that you might have. Is there anything that you'd like me to go over again?

Client: Did you say that I won't have to pay any taxes on the growth of these bonds?

FC: That's right. And they have almost twice the return that your current short-term CDs have. These are ideal selections if you are going to hold them until your children are ready for school. You know that the money will be there.

[Visual word.]

Client: Looks good to me.

[Justifies order size.]

FC: Great. A moment ago you reiterated that you wanted to invest $20,000 for each child at this time. Is that still the case?

Client: Yes.

[Asks for order.]

FC: Then, based upon that and the prices I quoted you, may I suggest that we place an order for $40,000 and $57,000 face of the bonds?

Client: Go ahead.

[Reads order back to customer.]
[Completes new account information.]

FC: Let me read the orders back to you. That's $40,000 face of the zero coupon, MBIA-insured Pennsylvania general obligation bonds of July 6, 19 __ (*8 years*) with a yield to maturity of 8½ percent; and $57,000 dollars face of the same bond maturing on July 6, 19 __ (*13 years*), with a yield to maturity of 9 percent. I've already got these bonds on hold for you. Let's take a moment and complete the new account information, and I'll confirm the order and call you back. All right?

Client: Good.

[The salesperson and the client complete the procedures to open the account.]

The Confirmation Call

[Confirms the customer's purchase, and makes arrangement for payment.]

FC: Dr. Jones? This is John Doe at XYZ. I'm just calling to tell you that we got the bonds at the price we agreed upon. You have five business days to pay for your purchase. Would you like to drop off a check or wire the money directly from your bank?

Client: I'll drop off a check on the way home from the hospital.

[Reminds the customer that he has done him a favor.]

FC: That's great! *Look,* I think we've made some excellent progress in *seeing* your children off to Harvard. Wouldn't you agree?

Client: Yes.

[Asks for a referral.]

FC: Before I go, can you think of anyone else who has kids going to college, or who is planning for retirement or paying too much in taxes, that I could help the same way?

[Shares referrals.]

Client: Why, yes, I guess I do. Both of my partners have children they'll be sending to college, and we're all in the Keogh together.

[Elicits the client's active cooperation in gaining the new prospects.]

FC: Thank you very much. Would you feel comfortable mentioning me to them? Then, when I call, it won't be out of the blue.

Client: That will be fine. I really appreciate your help, and I look forward to our meeting with my accountant. Thanks again. Good-bye.

This is an example of the development of the relationship between an FC and his client. As they continue to meet, the FC will build additional rapport and continue to elicit buying criteria.

MANAGING STRESS IN TODAY'S FINANCIAL MARKETPLACE

"Every day in every way . . . things are getting more and more stressful." At least, that's what most of us feel. Financial consultants have one of the most stressful jobs there is. In fact, stress-related burnout is probably the single greatest cause of failure among FCs, whose careers last only five years on average. But FCs aren't the only ones who find their job stressful.

According to pollster Louis Harris's recent book *Inside America,* 89 percent of all adult Americans (roughly 158 million people) report experiencing high levels of stress. Almost 60 percent say they feel "great stress" at least once or twice a week, and nearly one third (over 30 percent) report they are living with high stress every day.

Stress has been shown to be a major contributor to physical and mental illness (insurance companies and medical authorities indicate that over 75 percent of *all* time lost from work can be attributed to stress), family breakup, drug and alcohol abuse, and suicide. Many psychiatric authorities believe that stress is the major cause of most mental illnesses. Among high-stress jobs (e.g, police officers, firefighters, stockbrokers, insurance sales personnel, executives, and psychotherapists), stress may be the single greatest cause of physical and mental problems, especially divorce, suicide, and burnout.

Insurance studies have shown that the families of stockbrokers tend to submit claims for mental health services significantly more frequently than the norm. According to informal research studies, the divorce rate among brokers exceeds 85 percent, and some studies show brokers running number three behind dentists and psychotherapists for suicide! One million-dollar broker told us that of the sixteen men who had trained with him ten years ago, *all* had since been divorced at least once!

These are grim statistics, and considering the nature of the responsibilities of today's FC, it might be useful to explore stress and how to combat it.

In this section, we briefly discuss what stress is, what it does, and how to deal with it in order to avoid becoming one of those grim statistics.

CHAPTER 35

What Is Stress?

Probably the simplest way to define stress is as the amount of challenge you experience. Physiologically, stress can be defined as anything that moves your body out of a state of "homeostasis" (balance). Most authorities agree that stress results from feelings of losing control over events that affect our physical and emotional well-being and our sense of self-worth. If this is added to a gradual loss of hope that things will improve, we become stressed and are at risk for burnout.

As an FC, you have far greater control over many of the factors that affect your well-being than most people do. Even so, there are many events that affect you that you cannot control. Examples are the state of the economy, foreign competition, and interest rates.

To avoid or overcome the sense of helplessness in the face of things beyond your control, it is important for you to develop personal values concerning what is meaningful and important to you (see Chapter 4). Remember, stress suppresses your immune system, leaving you vulnerable to illness. In addition to potential physical ailments, you may also develop feelings of a loss of identity and self-esteem.

Do you know anyone who has performed well in the past but who seems to be losing his or her sales ability now? Someone who may even appear to have "given up"? How about someone who has become virtually obsessed with work and "trying to get ahead"? For many of us, stress can lead to feelings of anxiety, depression, and a sense of being driven. In our attempts to regain a sense of control, many of us cross the line from productive to self-destructive behaviors. What is most ironic is that stress is a self-induced wound.

Today we are constantly surrounded by reminders of what we have to own, look like, and accomplish to be considered "successful." If we accept advertising's concept of "success," we can easily develop feelings of inadequacy over failure to obtain it. This can lead to a sense of being trapped and the development of feelings of hopelessness and helplessness in trying to get what you "really want" out of life. According to Dr. Robert Eliot, a noted heart specialist, a far more important question to ask is, "Am I winning?" Also ask yourself whose standards you're using to determine that. Then scrutinize those standards and decide whether anyone could meet them.

Too many of us demand the impossible of ourselves and others. If you are impatient with anything short of perfection, you may be setting yourself up for "failure," frustration, and strong feelings of hopelessness.

Early Signs of Stress

Emotional Signs:

- *Apathy:* Can't seem to get your motor started.
- *Anxiety:* Worrying about what will go wrong next.
- *Irritability:* Short temper with family and peers.
- *Mental fatigue:* Sometimes it's just hard to think.
- *Overcompensation or denial:* What problems?
- *Feelings of helplessness:* "What can I do?"
- *Hopelessness:* "What's the use?"
- *Self-castigation:* "I never do anything right."
- *Confusion:* "I just don't know what to do."

Behavioral Signs:

- *Avoiding things:* Not making sales calls.
- *Doing things to extremes:* Making more calls than you can possibly follow up on.
- *Difficulty solving even simple administrative problems:* The simplest work becomes overwhelming.
- *Legal problems:* The temptation to take ''shortcuts.''
- *Loss of productivity.*

Physical Signs:

- *Excessive worry about, or denial of, illness*
- *Frequent illness:* It seems you always have a cold.
- *Physical exhaustion:* Always tired.
- *Reliance on self-medication:* Alcohol, illegal drugs, and over-the-counter medications.
- *Ailments:* Frequent feelings of ''not feeling good.''
- *Sleeplessness.*
- *Loss of appetite or weight:* Food becomes tasteless.
- *Chronic muscular aches:* Frequent back pain.
- *Accelerated heart rate:* Palpitations.
- *Accelerated respiration:* Can't catch your breath.
- *Tightness in the joints and muscles.*
- *Headaches.*
- *Stomach disorders:* Diarrhea, constipation, nausea.

The Cost of Stress

- *Skin problems:* Hives, lichen simplex, shingles.
- *Cardiovascular difficulties:* High blood pressure, migraine headaches, heart attack, stroke.
- *Gastrointestinal problems:* Ulcers, ulcerative colitis, constipation, diarrhea.
- *Genitourinary problems:* Difficulty urinating, impotence, frigidity.
- *Psychological problems:* Depression, anxiety.

Physiological Responses to Stress

Immediate Threat: The Alarm Response

When we first perceive a challenge as a threat to our physical well-being, sense of control, or self-esteem, we become alarmed and our body enters a defensive mode. In this mode, we tend to respond actively—by becoming angry or aggressive—and adrenaline is released into our bloodstream, causing:

- The heart to beat faster and stronger, resulting in a rapid rise in blood pressure.
- The blood to be shunted away from the stomach and skin to the muscles.
- The release of cholesterol into the bloodstream to provide energy.
- The blood to thicken to enable it to clot more easily in case of injury.
- The pupils to dilate, which enables us to see better.
- The hearing to become more acute.
- The enhancement of touch by the hairs on the body standing up (like the fur of an alerted animal).
- The senses of taste and smell to be enhanced.
- Sweating in order to cool the underlying muscles.
- The facial muscles to tense and the face to flush.
- The nostrils to flare, the throat and all the air passages in the lungs to dilate, breathing to quicken, and blood sugar to rise.
- Endorphins to be released from the hypothalamus to block pain.
- Sex hormones to be reduced.

After all these body functions take place, you are ready to fight or flee.

Long-Term Threat: Resistance and Exhaustion

When we feel threatened over a long period of time, our defenses enter a maintenance mode. In this mode, they keep us vigilant, hyperalert to additional threat to body or ego. We begin to feel that we've lost control of our lives. This sense of having lost control makes us feel passive, helpless to remove the threat, and hopeless of improvement. We begin to develop self-doubt and question our self-worth, becoming anxious and depressed. During this hyperalert period, cortisol is released and moves slowly through the body, causing:

- A slow rise in blood pressure, which, if maintained too high for too long, can lead to essential hypertension.
- Retention by the body tissues of vital body chemicals, such as salt.
- The release of cholesterol and clotting agents into the bloodstream, making it harder for the heart to pump.
- Repressed production of sex hormones (testosterone in the male and progesterone in the female).
- Increased production of gastric acid to maximize digestion.
- Impairment of the immune system's defenses against disease.
- Chronic arousal of the body's alertness.

If we remain out of control and threatened too long, we will reach a state of exhaustion in which we become totally unable to cope. This can result in mental breakdown, physical illness, or even death.

Hot Reactors

You may be wondering how all this talk about the effects of stress affects you. Dr. Robert Eliot, the author (with Dennis L. Breo) of *Is It Worth Dying For?*, has made a series of discoveries regarding the way our responses to situations affect our physical and mental health.

One of his discoveries is that some people respond in the same way to simple challenges (e.g., completing a billing form or figuring a commission) as they would be to a life-threatening situation. He refers to these individuals as **"Hot Reactors."** According to his research, almost one-fifth of all people who feel that they are under stress are Hot Reactors, and in some professions (e.g., top insurance salespeople), the number is as high as 40 percent.

If you are a Hot Reactor, you may experience the physical reactions of the "alarm" response to simple challenges forty or more times a day without even being aware of it. In some situations, your blood pressure may increase 100 percent. Subjecting your body to this kind of reaction on a constant basis will eventually cause it to break down.

Remember, if you feel threatened over a period of time, your body goes into the "resistance mode," adding cortisol to your system. Thus, when the alarm occurs again, your body's system begins its alert with higher levels of blood pressure, blood thickness, stomach acidity, and so forth. This addition of more adrenaline to a system already flush with cortisol can lead the heart muscles to literally tear themselves apart—one of the common findings in 87 percent of sudden cardiac death.

A Hot Reactor is harder to spot than a "Type A" personality. In fact, recent research by the American Medical Association indicates that there are just as many "Type B" Hot Reactors as "Type As."

Each year more than 1.2 million people suffer heart attacks. Over half of those heart attacks are caused by stress, and in nearly one-third of the attacks, the first symptom is **death!** That means that over 1,200 people die from stress-related heart attacks every day!

Stress attacks more than just the heart. Few people realize that stress is probably the single greatest cause of impotence in men and frigidity in women. Failure to recognize this and to discuss it openly and with understanding has hurt many marriages when one or both partners began to fear loss of their sexuality.

The Million Dollar Round Table

In 1985, Dr. Robert Eliot conducted a study with the members of the Million Dollar Round Table (the insurance industry's highest producers). He found that 39 percent were Hot

Reactors, and another 25 percent were undiagnosed hypertensives. That is, two out of three of the top producers in the insurance industry were in imminent cardiac danger. He also found that 80 percent felt that their lives were not fulfilling and were consequently unhappy.

These are grim numbers for anyone who wants to be successful in sales. However, there is a happy ending.

Dr. Eliot and his group worked with the participants in the study to help them learn how to deal with stress in their lives, and the results were phenomenal. **Six months later, all of the participants were healthy.** *None* were Hot Reactors and *none* were hypertensive. All reported that life had taken on new meaning and that meaning was good. In addition, the average workweek for these individuals had dropped from seventy hours to just forty to fifty hours. Best of all, the participants had significantly increased their production during the same period.

The year 1986 was a fantastic one for the insurance industry. On the average, members of the Million Dollar Round Table increased their production by 11 percent over the previous year. When Dr. Eliot did a follow-up of his test group in January 1987, he found that everyone was still healthy and happy. In addition, the smallest increase in production for a member of the group was 40 percent while the average increase was in excess of 100–200 percent over the previous year.

What this boils down to is proof that you *can* have it all. Success doesn't have to mean ulcers, heart attacks, and an early grave. In fact, it can mean just the opposite. **You can succeed and enjoy yourself while you do it!** All you have to do is learn how to handle stress in your life.

Managing Stress

Stress Isn't All Bad

We can balance all of its damaging side effects with the fact that stress, or challenge, isn't *all* bad. In fact, not enough challenge in your life can be as bad as too much. It can lead to apathy, lethargy, and a general feeling of unfulfillment, while just the right amount can help you grow to your fullest potential.

Effective **time management** is an important tool in coping with stress (see Chapter 4). Review your life for a moment and try to determine whether you have too much stress or not enough. If you have too many challenges (the most common complaint among salespeople), begin to learn to say "No," to additional responsibilities. You may even need to cut back on your current work load or social obligations.

However, if you don't have enough challenge in your life, begin to say "Yes" to additional challenges and responsibilities. You may find yourself not only with more to do, but also with more energy.

Make a list of your current activities. When you have completed it, determine which activities you are involved in because you really have to do them, which you're involved in because you really want to do them, and which you're involved in for any other reason. Then make a notation next to each for "Have to," "Want to," and "Neither." When you are done, start eliminating the activities that you've marked as "Neither" on your list.

Make a Plan

Hyrum Smith, the great time management expert, points out that no one can manage time. All we can do is manage the events that impinge upon us in time. To do this, write down those events and factors that have the most impact on you. Distinguish those that you can control (e.g., the number of sales calls you make) from those that you cannot control (e.g., the economy). Then develop and follow a plan to **take control of the things that you can control** and to lessen the impact upon you of the things that you can't control.

TAKE CONTROL OF THE EVENTS IN YOUR LIFE.

Attainable Goals

The importance of establishing attainable goals cannot be overemphasized. Without any goals, our behavior becomes directionless and lacks meaning. If we set goals that are unattainable, they will become a source of frustration and stress. The following five conditions are necessary to establish a well-formed goal (see Chapter 3 for more details):

1. State your goal in positive language: Write down what you want rather than what you don't want.
2. The goal must be within your control. If you are sixty years old, a goal of winning the decathon in the Olympics is obviously not within your control.

3. The goal should preserve your "ecology"—that is, attaining it should not cost you more than it's worth. We know of many millionaires who lost their families in gaining their "success" and who would gladly trade their millions to have them back again.

4. Be very specific both in describing your goal and in judging how you will know when you have achieved it. From your description, someone else should be able to recognize when you have reached your goal.

5. However you view your current state, there are probably many positive aspects about it. Unless your goal maintains these positive aspects, you may find yourself unconsciously defeating your efforts to obtain the goal.

Once you have established your intermediate and long-term goals, break them down into daily increments. Each day set yourself a goal that you can attain, and then reward yourself for attaining it. The nature of the reward is up to you (watching a ball game, reading a novel, a treat, etc.), but see that you earn and enjoy a little reward every day. You'll be surprised what this does for your attitude.

Point of View

One interesting result of studies on stress management is that far more important than the actual events in your life is the way you interpret those events and the meaning that you assign them. Dr. Viktor Frankl in his book *Man's Search for Meaning,* speaks of his years in a Nazi extermination camp. While there, he frequently tried to determine which prisoners might survive and which would be unable to cope. At first he based his determinations on the youth and physical strength of the prisoners, but too frequently, young, healthy prisoners would come into the barracks and announce that they had given up. The next day they were found dead in their bunks. When they lost the will to live, they died!

Others (many in their forties and fifties), who were not in

top physical condition, survived. Despite all the odds against them, they were still alive when the camp was liberated four years later. Frankl determined that there was one great factor separating those who gave up and died from those who held on until they were liberated. That factor was the "meaning" people assigned to their lives and to the events that occurred.

Dr. Frankl says that if life has meaning, then all suffering also has meaning and can be borne, no matter how great. But if life is meaningless, then all suffering is meaningless and is unbearable, no matter how small. Remember, it is not the event that causes stress, it is the meaning that we assign to the event.

When something doesn't go your way, do you interpret it as a failure, proof that you are unworthy? Or do you look for what you can learn from the experience? One of the great blessings of "failing," is that it makes people more willing to try something different.

What's Your Point of View?

Ask yourself, "What is the meaning of my life?" If you are not sure, think about it. How would you like to be remembered after you are gone? Do you want to be remembered for being a "million-dollar producer," or are there other, more important things?

Thoughts versus Feelings

Perhaps Solomon said it best over 4,000 years ago: "As a man thinketh, so is he." **What you think about, and how you think about it (the meaning that you assign to events), determine how you feel and the impact that the event will have on your health.** Try this simple excercise:

> Relax and get as comfortable as you can. Take a deep breath, hold it for a slow count of three, and let it out. Now think back and remember the happiest moment of your life (perhaps the day you got married, your third birthday party, or when the

doctor handed you your new child to hold for the first time). Try to really get into the memory; rather than seeing yourself doing something, feel yourself doing it. Reexperience everything as if you were actually there and reliving it. Do this for about one minute and then return.

How do you feel? Pretty good? Now do the same thing, but this time relive a moment of minor irritation such as a traffic delay, getting "bawled out" for something, or missing an important putt in a golf game. Again, relive the experience for about one minute, and then return.

How do you feel now? Not so good? Finally, return to the happiest moment of your life. Again, relive it as it was then and make it real. Do this for one moment and then return. Notice how good you feel. What you thought about determined how you felt.

Now, take a three-by-five card and on one side of it write down ten qualities you possess that others might find admirable or attractive (e.g., your concern for others, your professionalism). On the other side, write down five of the happiest moments of your life and five successes in your life (times when you felt that you could do anything, overcome any obstacle, such as winning a race or "acing" a course in school).

Carry the card with you, and the next time that you feel discouraged, take it out and read your good qualities. Remind yourself that you are a good, competent person. Then turn it over, relax, and relive each of the ten moments you've written there for one minute apiece. Before you complete number five, you will find that you have completely regained your confidence and positive outlook. By following these methods, you can **take control of how you feel!**

TAKE CONTROL OF HOW YOU FEEL.

Humor

Developing a good sense of humor, and the ability to laugh at ourselves and the situations in which we find ourselves, is one of the easiest and most effective ways to regain control of the impact that circumstances have on our feelings. It also lets us see our circumstances from a different point of view (humorous instead of ego- or life-threatening). In their book, *Frogs into Princes,* Richard Bandler and John Grinder point out that since we often say to ourselves, "Someday I'll probably look back on all this and laugh," *why wait?!* Laugh now instead of letting circumstances overwhelm you.

Mickey Mouse

Is there someone at the office, or elsewhere, who upsets you even to think about? Take a moment to mentally picture that person. As you do, endow him with ears like Mickey Mouse and a beak and voice like Donald Duck's. Does he still upset you? Change other things about the person until thinking about him doesn't bother you. With a little practice, every time you meet that person, you'll see Mickey Mouse and hear Donald Duck.

> LAUGH NOW AND AVOID THE STRESS.

Helping Your Family to Help You

Your family can either be a lifesaving support or an additional source of threat. Nearly 26 percent of all sudden cardiac deaths occur on Monday mornings. An additional 25 percent occur on Saturday mornings. These are the times when we switch from one source of stress to another.

There are several easy steps that you can take that will help you not only to cope with stress in your own life, but also to avoid becoming a source of stress for your family and co-workers.

Keep Your Balance

Anyone can lift and carry two to three times more weight if it is well balanced than if it is unbalanced. This is also true of psychic burdens such as stress.

To really cope with the complexities of today's world, we must develop and maintain a sense of inner balance among our mental, physical, emotional, career, social, and spiritual selves. If any one of these is overemphasized at the expense of the others, it can leave us without the resources to fully cope when we are under pressure.

Prepare for Change

In the competitive arena of sales, change is inevitable and constant. To deal with change, we must learn to anticipate it and prepare for its impact upon our lives and our families.

If you are new to your job (especially if you are involved in management or sales), the odds are high that your family and loved ones are not prepared for the changes that will occur in their lives as a result of your career change. Be certain that you discuss your job with them regularly. In addition, you should discuss not only your own goals for your career but also *their* goals for your career. After all, you are asking them to support your work.

One of the primary changes that your family will have to deal with is your work hours. To succeed in your new job, especially if you are a manager or an FC, you may need to work at least two or three nights per week for several years. If your family and loved ones are not already familiar with such a work pattern, this can be a severe disruption. Even if you have already told them and they seemed understanding and supportive, don't be lulled into a false sense of security. Until they have actually experienced the change, they won't really know what kind of impact it will have on them.

Once you have established a pattern (e.g., your "being there" every night), it is natural for those close to you to unconsciously expect that pattern to continue. They develop further patterns of meeting their needs around that pattern, and when you change, it affects them. Imagine the typical family of five as pictured in Exhibit 36-1.

Each circle represents a family member; the lines connecting the circles represent relationships among the family members, and those extending beyond the circles represent rela-

EXHIBIT 36-1

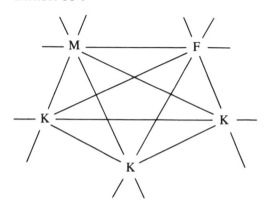

tionships between each member and their outside commitments (work, friends, church, etc.). Notice what happens in Exhibit 36-2 when one member changes his or her accepted role (e.g., begins a new job, becomes an adolescent, etc.). The relationships stretch, producing tension (and stress) in *all* of the relationships in the family.

EXHIBIT 36-2

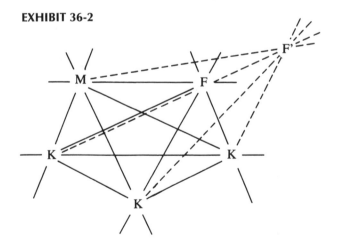

There are only three ways to reduce those tensions.

1. Best and hardest is for the family to work together to adjust to the change (see Exhibit 36-3). Your family's effectiveness in

EXHIBIT 36-3

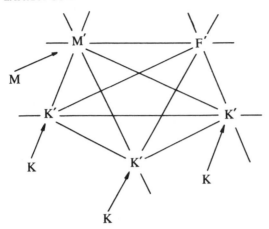

doing this can radically affect their ability to cope with stress in their lives. If this does not occur, you may find that the tension you bring home from work shows up in your children's poor grades or behavior in school.

2. The family can exert so much pressure upon the person who has changed that that person changes back (e.g., quits the new job), as in Exhibit 36-4. This occurs because your family, like your body, is a system, and no system can tolerate tension for very long. As a result, it always moves to reduce that tension.

EXHIBIT 36-4

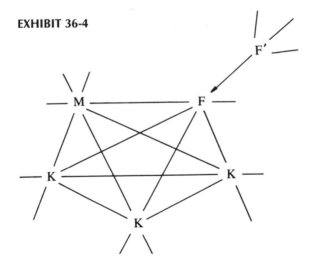

This is one reason why so many alcoholics have difficulty staying sober: Once their families have adjusted to the individual as an alcoholic, they resist the further adjustment needed to cope with the individual sober. They will subtly pressure him to drink again.

3. The most tragic way to adjust occurs when the family system cannot cope with the tension any longer (see Exhibit 36-5) and "cuts" the relationships to the stress-producing individual. This can result in divorce, suicide, murder, running away, alcohol and drug abuse, or mental illness.

EXHIBIT 36-5

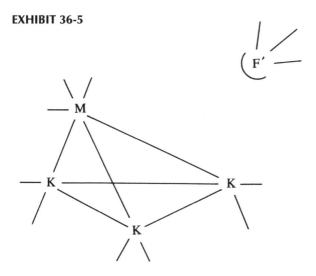

Keep Courting

What can you do to avoid having your family see your job as a rival for your time and attention? **Court your spouse *and* your children.** For many couples, the courtship ends as soon as they have said "I do." Everyone needs to feel courted, needed, and loved. Therefore, make sure that the time you do spend with your loved ones is "quality time." This is time in which your main objective is to meet your family's needs. This isn't easy since it requires you to devote your total attention to others for periods of time.

If you work two to three nights per week, suggest that your spouse bring the children to work at six, and then go out to eat as a family. This way you can see your family, release office tension, and then return to your office feeling more satisfied with your accomplishments. In addition, it helps the children to see your late nights as potentially fun instead of dreary. When dinner is over, take one of the children back to the office and let him or her use the desk next to yours to do homework.

If your children are teenagers, let them help you with chores such as stuffing envelopes, so they feel that they are part of the effort to reach family goals. If they are older teenagers, and if your manager approves, it may be possible for them to cold-call potential customers for you. When the ''work'' evening is over, stop for a treat, such as ice cream, together on the way home. By having the children take turns, you can have a special experience with a different child each week.

If possible, have your spouse join you alone for dinner once a week. After dinner, both of you can do whatever work you've brought home from the office at desks next to one another. If you spouse hasn't any work, ask him or her to help you in some of your tasks. At the very least, your spouse can keep you company by watching television nearby.

Call your spouse to go out on a real date together once a week. The nature of the date will be far less important than the anticipation of it.

Family Council

Hold a family council each week to discuss all family members' progress toward *their* goals. Find out their needs and discuss their responsibilities, their goals, and any help they desire from other family members. Remember, it is important to keep such meetings as free from tension as possible—unreasonable goals should not be encouraged.

Mail a note home to your spouse and each of your children once a week (or slip the note into their lunch or a pocket) telling them that you are thinking of them. Bring home a surprise that you think they will like to let them know they're special to you. It doesn't take a lot of money to say "I love you," but it can be very important.

Loving Memories

Last of all, always try to make going home a reward to yourself. Don't let family problems overwhelm your family's beneficial effect on you. Have you ever experienced a time of great difficulties with a family member? Have you dreaded going home because you knew there would be a "fight"? One way to alleviate this dread is to take a moment before leaving work to relax at your desk, close your eyes, and remember a loving moment shared with that family member. If the problem is with your spouse, remember and relive how you felt the day you got engaged. If the problem is with a child, remember and relive how you felt the first time the doctor handed him or her to you as an infant. You'll be surprised at how unimportant "problems" and misunderstandings become, and as you change, so will your loved one.

Family and friends can either increase your level of stress or reduce it. It is up to you which happens. Take the time to strengthen your support groups.

Positive Mental Attitude

In computer terminology, "GIGO means, "garbage in—garbage out." Your brain is the most sophisticated computer known, yet this rule applies to it as well. Each day little discouragements, news items, business changes, and rejections from prospects or customers fill you brain with negative information. All around you are people and circumstances telling you that you can't win and there's no point in trying. Even if you don't listen to them with your conscious mind, your unconscious mind picks up these negatives, and after a while, even the most optimistic person can become discouraged. When you feel discouraged, pull out the three-by-five card we discussed earlier to raise your spirits. But also avoid letting self-doubt dampen your spirits in the first place. In fact, programming your mind to think positively will help you.

"PMA" Books

Your local bookstore has hundreds of excellent books on maintaining a positive mental attitude (see the bibliography at the end of this book). Most say the same thing in different ways: Remember, **you are a winner, and you can accomplish anything that you set your mind to!**

Read a chapter each morning before you go to work to program yourself for success. If you have a rough morning, read another chapter during lunch. Finally, read a chapter before going to bed (reading this aloud with your spouse can be excellent for a marriage). Psychologists have found that the last thing you think about before you go to sleep programs your unconscious for the remainder of the night. If you go to bed worried and upset, you will spend the night that way and wake up suffering from the "Wrong Side of the Bed Syndrome." Why not program yourself to wake up with the "Right Side of the Bed Syndrome?" Then you can spend the rest of the day feeling good, despite any unimportant setbacks that occur.

"PMA" Tapes

Another aid in maintaining a positive mental attitude is the audiotape that carries the same messages as your chosen book. You can listen to it while commuting or getting dressed in the morning. The important thing is to take control over what gets programmed into your mind by consciously choosing to fill your mind with positive ideas.

Work Environment

Remember, *always* eat away from your desk. The unconscious mind tends to label areas as work areas, play areas, eating areas, and so on. Moreover, customers and operations centers are put off by materials that are sticky or have coffee cup rings on them.

Eating away from your desk is particularly important at lunchtime. Trying to eat while dealing with the stress of calls from customers or other managers is a very effective way to give yourself heartburn, if not gastritis, ulcer, or worse. Leave the office behind you and go to lunch somewhere where you won't even think about work. Recharge your batteries. Read a book. After lunch, go window shopping or take a brisk walk. Studies have shown that these kinds of breaks can radically increase your effectiveness after lunch, while thinking about your office problems through your lunch hour can leave you ineffective and exhausted by the end of the day.

You should also try to avoid the office crank. Almost every office seems to have one individual who thinks that the world will end tomorrow. Be pleasant, but make it known that you're not interested in talking about negative things.

The important thing to remember is that you are in control of your life and your health.

TAKE CONTROL OF YOUR LIFE.

CHAPTER 37

Your Body and Stress

Change Your Stress

When people work all day at a desk, they often can't just sit down and relax when they get home. If you find this happening to you, the first step to overcoming the stress is to change its nature. If you've been working on mental problems, do something physical like playing tennis or taking a walk. Afterward you will be able to relax more easily, if for no other reason than that you have burned off some of the stress chemicals stored up in your body during the day. (*Note:* The physical activity should be something you *enjoy* doing.)

Eat Right

There are many excellent books available on diet and stress. You may also consult your physician about a diet. In any case, a safe rule of thumb is to always eat intelligently and avoid extremes. Be sure to get plenty of fiber, and concentrate on complex carbohydrates such as vegetables. Finally, eat because you are hungry, not because you are tired, working, or watching television.

Exercise

Exercise is also a matter of moderation and intelligence. Handled properly, it not only burns off stress chemicals but also raises your metabolic set point and burns off excess weight.

Before beginning an exercise program, be sure to check with your doctor to determine what is appropriate for you. Then find an activity you enjoy and do it three to five times a week, working your way up gradually to thirty minutes a session.

In school, the coaches used to tell us, "No pain, no gain." This is *not* true. When your body hurts, it is trying to tell you something important, and you should listen to it. If you are exercising and it hurts, *stop!* Cool down gradually and call it a day.

Tobacco

Of the 50 million people who smoke, one-half to two-thirds will die simply because they smoke. If you could distill all of the nicotine, arsenic, strychnine, and tar from a single cigarette and inject it into your vein, you would be dead before you could reach the door to call for help.

Ninety-eight percent of all smokers are *addicted* to nicotine. Nicotine plus carbon monoxide makes a deadly combination. The nicotine speeds up the heart and forces it to work harder, while the carbon monoxide robs the heart of the oxygen it needs, slowly strangling it.

When the body becomes stressed, the air sacs in the lungs expand to increase the amount of oxygen to the body. If you smoke when you are under stress, you cause up to ten times the damage to your lungs as you would smoking when you are relaxed. Women who smoke while on birth control pills run even higher risks of developing or aggravating hardening of the arteries, blood clotting (which can lead to stroke or heart attack), and heart disease.

Alcohol

Among the many damaging side effects caused by alcohol, the following are some of the most serious.

- It stimulates production of the stress hormone cortisol.
- It is a diuretic (it dries you out) and therefore enhances the body's clotting mechanisms.
- It directly damages heart fibers, over time causing the heart to become weak and flabby.
- Alcohol kills brain cells.
- It causes cirrhosis of the liver, which is the fourth-largest killer of middle-aged men.
- It causes alcoholic hypertension.
- It creates temporary, reversible damage of the bone marrow.
- Alcohol puts pregnant women at special risk and can cause fetal alcohol syndrome.
- It significantly increases the chance of breast cancer in women.
- Alcohol contains empty calories.

Caffeine

Coffee and tea, two popular "safe" drinks that contain the stimulant caffeine, actually have many harmful side effects. These include:

- Caffeine releases adrenaline.
- It aggravates stress.
- It can cause irritability and anxiety attacks.
- It hinders restful sleep.

KEEP YOURSELF FIT TO COPE WITH STRESS.

Summary

In this section, we discussed the nature of stress, its potential impact upon your health, and ways to minimize its negative effects. Remember that change is inevitable. By planning and preparing for it, you will be better able to maintain a sense of balance in your life. Develop a sense of humor and the ability to ''look back with laughter'' on a trying circumstance now instead of waiting a few years to enjoy its comical aspects.

> YOU'RE IN CONTROL.

APPENDICES

Mastery Exercises

Exercise 1: Psychological Profiling (See Chapters 9 through 13)

Read each of the following paragraphs, and decide which psychological profile the individual described or speaking would fit into: Executive, Socialite, Bureaucrat, or Dictator. (The answers follow immediately.)

1. "We all know just how important it is to perform exactly as is expected—no more and no less. A company ought to get what it pays for, and it doesn't pay us to make up new company policies."

   _____

2. "A department runs efficiently if all its people are working in accord with one another. This virtually ensures that the company is getting optimal performance."

   _____

3. "The company requires that you pay attention to both the needs of the individual and the objectives of the department.

Neither should always be paramount.''

---

4. "There can be one captain of a ship and one captain only. When I want your opinion, I'll ask for it. Till then, just do what I tell you. After all, I've been through this type of situation before.''

---

5. This person's office has pictures of various teams that he has been on and snapshots of family members, as well as mementoes of every office party he ever attended. The placement of the desk chair is designed for easy, casual conversation.

---

6. This person's office is rather stark and bare. The desk chair has a high back and is arranged opposite and slightly above the visitor's chair.

---

7. This person's office is somewhat stark but has company-oriented mementoes and plaques and awards placed throughout. It seems to be utilitarian.

---

8. This person's office is stuffed to the gills with papers that are scattered and unbelievably messy. His organizational system consists of remembering approximately on which side of the office something is located.

---

9. "I wonder where all the competent people went to. The only way to get something done right is to do it yourself.''

---

10. "I know that management and the union are seemingly on opposite sides of the fence. Let's get everybody together to see how we can resolve the situation for our mutual benefit.''

Answers to Exercise 1

1. Bureaucrat, because of the need to perform exactly as expected and not to modify policies.
2. Socialite, because of the emphasis on interpersonal relationships as the primary determinant of effectiveness.
3. Executive, because of the realization that there are two sides to the issue.
4. Dictator, because of the need for individualized command.
5. Socialite, because of the emphasis on group activities.
6. Dictator, because of the control implications of the seating arrangement.
7. Probably an Executive, although the description is too vague to be certain. Remember, people are not always easy to categorize immediately.
8. Again, the information is too vague to categorize this person.
9. Dictator, because of the implication that the speaker is the only competent person.
10. Executive, because of the realization that there are two sides that deserve attention.

Exercise 2: Sensory Words (See Chapter 17)

Read each of the following and decide which sensory mode is being used. (The answers follow immediately.)

1. "Let's take a look at all sides of the proposal and decide which avenue is most attractive."

   _____

2. "What we have here is a failure to communicate. Everyone's always talking about what they want, but they never seem to get it down on paper. Talk is cheap, but let me have some time to study the figures. Then I'll know whether or not I'm interested."

   _____

3. "Did you ever get the sense that they don't know exactly what's coming down? They move their mouths, but seem to be missing the entire idea."

_____

4. "I think that we should consider the proposal very carefully. There are numerous points that need to be pondered."

_____

Answers to Exercise 2

1. Visual.
2. This person has both an auditory and a visual orientation. The need to *see it* is a dominant theme.
3. Kinesthetic.
4. Unspecified.

Exercise 3: (see Chapter 17)

Choose the best response for the following statement. (Answer follows immediately.)

"After I look over the literature, I want to speak with a few people who already own the product. Based upon how satisfied they are, I'll know whether the literature is telling the truth."

A. Let me show you some information that you should find interesting. Then I'll relate some comments from satisfied customers that should help.

B. I'm sure that you'll get a good feeling once you read over the literature. There are a lot of excellent things that people are saying.

C. After you get a sense of what is going on, I'll show you a few things that will make you feel even better.

D. I can see that once you read some of the literature, you'll be able to make a decision based on a positive gut reaction.

Answer to Exercise 3

A is the best response.

Exercise 4: Sensory Words, Criteria, and Personality Styles (See Chapters 14 and 17)

Read each of the following. Circle the sensory words and underline the key criteria for determining the individual's personality type. (The answers follow immediately.)

1. "I want to get a feel for the proposal to ensure that it doesn't diverge too significantly from standard operating procedure. I know that this has been important to you, but I don't want too much decentralization. You know what happened to our archrival. He let things get out of control and subsequently lost significant market share to me—I mean, us. It made me laugh for weeks. But there's no way that'll happen here. I'll personally attend to that if I have to make them toe the line myself."

2. "Most of us have decided that it would be a good idea to attend the lecture on stress management. You know how it's important to the company that we learn as much as we can about it. Anyway, it will be a good chance to get together."

3. "Numerous factors have led to the creation of this new administration. The people have decided that they want to have the control necessary to positively affect their destinies."

4. "I chose this company because of its reputation for reliability. I've heard many good things about it over the years, and it seems that it warrants those comments. Over time, I've become more familiar with it and find that the assistance that I've received conforms to the level of service that should be provided."

5. "My friends know that this is the right place to go. This is the

most popular club in town. You can just tell from the feel of the place. Everyone else comes here and I have to maintain my image.''

Answers to Exercise 4

[Sensory words are set in all capitals.]

1. "I want to get a FEEL for the proposal to ensure it *doesn't diverge too significantly from standard operating procedure*. I know that this has been important to you, but I *don't want too much decentralization*. You know what happened to our archrival. He let things get out of *control* and subsequently lost significant market share to me—I mean, us. It made me laugh for weeks. But, there's no way that'll happen here. I'll personally attend to that if I have to make them TOE THE LINE myself.''

    > This person is a Dictator because of the emphasis on me/myself/I. The obvious need to take control and disregard for other people further reinforce this. Kinesthetic words/phrases have been capitalized. Key motivations have been underlined. In this situation, the person doesn't want other people to diverge from the standard operating procedures that *he* initiated. Control and the fear of decentralization (giving up some control) reinforce this point.

2. *"Most of us have decided* that it would be a good idea to attend the lecture on stress management. You know how *it's important to the company* that *we* learn as much as *we* can about it. Anyway, *it will be a good chance to get together*.''

    > Socialite.

3. "Numerous factors have led to the creation of this new administration. *The people have decided that they want to have the control necessary to positively affect their destinies*.''

    > Possibly a Socialite, but could also be an Executive. Control is the key motivation, with the positive influencing of the future at a major point. You would probably sell to this person by emphasizing the fulfillment of a future wish and using a "people orientation."

4. "I chose this company because of its reputation for *reliability*. I've HEARD many good things about it over the years, and it seems that it warrants those COMMENTS. *Over time,* I've become more familiar with it and find that the *assistance* that I've received conforms to the *level of service* that should be provided."

> Note the auditory words. Note also that in the key motivations *reliability* and *over time* tend to go together. Reliability is partly a function of quality over a period of time. Assistance and service are also similar concepts.

5. "My friends know that this is the *right place to go*. This is *the most popular* club in town. You can just TELL FROM THE FEEL OF THE PLACE. *Everyone else* COMES HERE and I have to *maintain my image*."

> This poor, mostly kinesthetic Socialite is a groupie.

Exercise 5: Regarding Key Motivations
(See Chapter 19)

Read the next three paragraphs and underline the themes that have the greatest frequency. (The answers follow immediately.)

A. "I chose this company to work for because it has an excellent reputation for quality. Everything it does indicates that. The fact that it offers many career paths is also important to someone like me, who is upwardly mobile. It's also the best-known company of its kind in the world."

B. "There's a great restaurant down the street that I'm sure you'll enjoy. It has a large menu that always gets rave reviews from the few of us who know about it."

C. "I like people who have a lot of different interests because it makes them interesting to talk to. But, more than anything, I must know that I can turn my back on them without fear."

Answers to Exercise 5

A: "I chose this company to work for because it has an excellent *reputation for quality*. Everything it does indicates that. The fact that it offers *many career paths* is also important to someone like me, who is *upwardly mobile*. It's also the *best-known* company of its kind in the world."

B: "There's a great restaurant *down the street* that I'm sure you'll enjoy. It has a *large menu* that always gets *rave reviews* from the *few of us who know about it*."

C: "I like people who have *a lot of different interests* because it makes them interesting to talk to. But, more than anything, I must know that I can *turn my back on them* without fear."

This person has *variety* (multiple career paths, large menu, many interests) as a key motivation. Additionally, the issue of "trust" is evident ("reputation for quality," "rave reviews," "turn my back on them"). "Down the street" may indicate a location issue, but this issue is evident only once.

Additional Sources of Prospecting Lists

Finding a good prospect list is mostly a matter of imagination and persistence. Remember, the greater the number of your potential prospects, the greater your chances of opening qualified accounts. In addition to the sources provided below, you should consider using list companies that, for a fee, will provide thousands of prospects who meet whatever criteria you specify. However, there are several important things to consider before using a list company:

- Whatever list you find, you will probably not be the first person to use it. Is that bad? Definitely not. Remember, someone who already has a broker is almost, by definition, qualified.

- Look in the *Yellow Pages* under "Mailing Lists" for list companies that have information about your area.

- Before you order a list, write down the characteristics of your "ideal" client. Give those characteristics to the list company and they will sort their records for individuals meeting your criteria—for example, every family with an annual income over $50,000 who had a baby within the last twelve months.

- Every additional criterion will incrementally increase the expense of purchasing a list. Specifying several criteria allows you to really "know" your prospects, but can lead to unnecessary expense if you overdo it. So review your criteria to make sure that each item is really necessary. By doing this you will significantly increase your efficiency without breaking your bankbook.

• Never throw away a name on a list. If you are unsuccessful in prospecting someone, try again in six months, or trade his or her name for another prospect with someone in your office. Each of you may have greater success with the other's prospect.

• Finally, you may further increase the efficiency of your lists by mailing a letter to all the prospects. Use the letter to inform them of your service(s) or product(s), and offer them the chance to write or call for additional information. Those who do write or call have proved their interest and will provide "warm" instead of "cold" calls for you. Call them first, then call those who did not respond. You can even begin by asking the latter if they got your letter.

Below is a brief list of other sources of potential prospects:

Directories:

1. Alumni lists and yearbooks
2. Classified business directory
3. Classified phone directory
4. Commercial ratings
5. Contractors' and builders' exchanges
6. Corporation register
7. County histories
8. *Directory of Directories*
9. Dun & Bradstreet
10. Files and title companies
11. Grain exchange
12. Labor unions
13. License bureaus
14. Livestock exchange
15. Mercantile reports
16. Mortgage lists
17. Medical professional associations
18. Office building directories
19. Professional directories
20. Teachers/college professors
21. Trade directories
22. Voters' lists
23. *Who's Who*

24. *Social Register* and *Blue Book*

Newspapers:

25. Building permits
26. Changes in business management
27. Changes in position
28. Contributors to charities
29. Executors of estates
30. Incorporation announcements
31. Marriage announcements
32. People selling expensive automobiles
33. People selling their businesses
34. People who have won lawsuits
35. Political appointments
36. Probates of wills
37. Promotions
38. Real estate sales
39. Society items
40. Professional athletes
41. Editors of local or farm newspapers

Membership Lists

42. Athletic clubs
43. Advertising clubs
44. Building and loan societies
45. Cemeteries
46. Chamber of commerce
47. Churches
48. Credit card companies
49. Credit unions
50. Colleges
51. Rotary, Kiwanis, and other service clubs
52. Schools
53. Social, musical clubs
54. Dinner clubs
55. Automobile clubs

Miscellaneous:

56. Agents
57. Addressing companies
58. Accountants, auditors
59. Bank officials
60. Brokers (real estate)
61. Farmers
62. Government officials
63. Investment reports
64. Moody's
65. Personal contacts
66. Successful sales personnel in other lines
67. Trade magazines
68. Year-end reports of companies

Openers for Cold Calling

This appendix contains additional generic and product-oriented openers.

Generic

FC: "Hello, my name is _____ from the investment firm of _____."

1. "The reason for my call is that my manager has personally asked me to give you a call. We are creating a mailing list for individuals such as yourself in one of three areas: growth, income, or tax-advantaged income. Which would you prefer to be on?"

(*Note:* Regardless of the response—growth, income, tax-advantaged income, or none—your next question is "Why?" In answering, the prospect will be qualifying himself.)

2. "We are starting a special service in this area. We are creating a list of people to whom we can send information on good investment ideas. Would you like to be on the list?"

3. "I know you're busy and I would like to send you information that is pertinent to your situation. Please tell me a bit about your investment objectives."

4. "The recent tax law changes have created a need for portfolio evaluation. I'd like to offer you the services of my firm in helping you determine just how you and your investments will fare in light of the recent changes."

5. "Recent economic changes have created a need for portfolio evaluation. I'd like to offer you the services of my firm in helping you determine just how you and your investments will fare in light of the recent changes."

(*Note:* The key idea here is to take whatever change is being currently discussed in the media—economic, tax, political, etc.—and use it as the rationale for the call. In essence, the media have done some of your advertising for you.)

6. "College education costs are skyrocketing. How are you planning to fund your child's education?"

(*Note:* This is particularly useful if you know that the prospect has children. You may have obtained this information from a list that you purchased. See Appendix 2.)

7. "As you probably know, we're very positive about the outlook for the economy. And, in line with this belief, we are committed to providing investors with the resources to effectively compete in the upcoming financial boom. Are you concerned about your financial future?"

8. "Many of the clients share a common concern about paying taxes. Are taxes a problem for you?"

9. "The most critical decisions we have to make today are frequently money decisions. Because of inflationary concerns, it is crucial that you manage your money appropriately. Has this been a concern of yours? Have you addressed it?"

10. "Would you agree that the more knowledge you have about investing, the greater your chances of being able to make wise decisions?"

11. "As you know, the end of the year is fast approaching. Do you think you're taking full advantage of the tax laws to reduce your tax liability?"

Product-Specific/Sales-Specific Openers

12. "Good morning, Dr. _____. This is _____ from _____ calling. I know you're very busy so I won't take up much of your time. I've recently come across some municipal bonds that have been very interesting to my other physician clients from a tax savings standpoint and that could also be of significant benefit to you."

13. "Mr. _____, I am making it a point to reach successful businessmen in our community who are probably interested in real estate—both as an investment and as a way to save tax dollars. I believe I may be able to show you a number of ways to invest in types of real estate without the major risks and discomforts normally associated with it, while also providing a significant return on investment."

14. "Ms. _____, in my experience, businesses such as yours generally have periods when all their capital is not in use. If you are presently leaving your short-term dollars in a savings account for those periods, I may be able to show you a number of alternative investments that would offer you better rates of return."

15. "Mr. _____, I am making it a point to reach families in your community who are interested in having funds available to meet the future educational needs of their children. I believe I can show you a number of ways to invest the dollars you want to allocate today for those future needs."

16. "With your impending retirement from _____ I'm sure you're taking another look at your financial objectives. Someone of your stature must be thinking now about how to maximize his retirement income. My company has a number of investments that may be suitable for you."

17. "I want to talk to you for just a minute about an investment that is commission-free, has a tax-free yield, and offers good

safety of principal. What are your present investments with those qualities?''

18. ''Since you and your husband are both working professionals, I would like to offer you some investment suggestions to significantly lower your tax burden. Do you have any provisions to do this?''

Responses to Prospecting Stalls and Objections

While you are prospecting, you will find that many people automatically respond with a stall or an objection to your call. These initial negative responses are very automatic and are akin to what many people say when approached by a sales clerk in a clothing store—"Just looking" or its equivalent.

You have two basic alternatives when you hear such a response: You can either hang up and dial the next number, or you can try to overcome the objection. Approximately nine out of every ten prospects will offer an objection. Financial consultants have found that two or three of the nine objections can be overcome merely by providing a standard response. Thus they are able to qualify 30 to 40 percent of their prospects rather than a mere 10 percent.

We think it's a shame that some sales courses suggest that you hang up as soon as you hear any "resistance." It is a terrible waste of time and energy to do this. Since you've already spent the time obtaining the phone number, dialing it, and giving an initial opening, you may as well go one step further and try to respond to a prospect's programmed, but basically meaningless, negative response.

This appendix alerts you to some typical initial negative responses and provides some standard answers to them.

I'm not in the market right now.
I'm not interested.
I have no money.

> *FC:* The chances of me calling you at a time when you actually had an interest/money are rather remote. The reason for my call is to find out how we may be of future service to you. What are your investment objectives?

The market is too high.
The market is too low.
The market is too risky.

> *FC:* You've obviously been studying the market to make that comment. Please tell me the factors that caused you to make this statement.

Or:

> *FC:* You may be right. Why do you say that?

I already have a broker.
I have a friend in the business.

> *FC:* Great. How have you been doing?

Or:

> *FC:* Good. Many of my best clients had another brokerage relationship before they decided to work with me. Which firm are you dealing with? How have you been doing? Et cetera.

Or:

> *FC:* Fine, most of my better customers have several brokers. No one in this business has a corner on all the good ideas. I am

confident that my company and I can provide you with superior service, and I'll let you judge for yourself.

I'm too busy to talk right now.

FC: I'm sorry to have called at such a bad time. Would you prefer that I call this afternoon at _____, or would tomorrow morning be better?

Send me your card.

FC: I'd be happy to. As long as I'm mailing it, I'd like to enclose a sample of our research. What type of securities do you normally buy?

What are you selling?
Are you trying to sell me something?

FC: Myself and my firm, Mr. _____. We'd like to handle your investment business.

I've been burnt before.
I'm already holding the "Losers" other brokers recommended.

FC: Well, it may pay to investigate what our research thinks about your best course of action. We might discover some viable alternative course of action. What are you holding right now?

I never buy stocks.
I have never bought stocks.

FC: That's interesting. May I ask you why you haven't?

Or:

FC: What alternative investments have you been purchasing?

I'm not interested.

FC: If you are not interested, then I must assume that you are successfully dealing with inflationary risk. Can you tell me how you've solved this problem?

How long have you been a broker?

FC: _____ years, but I don't pretend to be an expert on the market or any group of securities. No one person can be. I feel that my primary obligation to you is twofold. First, to act as a liaison between you and our research department, keeping you abreast of its opinions on your holdings; and second, to present you with the facts and information about the market when they occur.

What can you do for me?

FC: My best. And that means a lot. Most people don't really know what to expect from a broker. I think you want as much interest and effort from me as you can get, but you don't want me bothering you unless it could be good for you. I'll do my best to give you all the service and interest you want without wasting your time.

Profiling Questions

General

What are your current investment needs?

What are you doing to meet your investment objectives?

What would you like your money to do for you and your family?

What do you expect from your broker?

What is your risk tolerance?

What are your plans for the future?

Where would you like to be in five years?

What is your major financial concern?

How much might you put into an investment that met all of your criteria?

What are your criteria for an investment decision?

What is your primary investment objective?

What investments have you made in the past?

What do you do with your savings dollars?

Why did you invest in the past?

How have your previous investments done?

What is your investment philosophy?

Have you ever invested in tax-advantaged investments?

What are your financial objectives for the short term? Intermediate term? Long term? Retirement?

What kind of investments are you currently involved with?

What is your taxable income?

Are there any financial questions I can answer for you?

Key Questions

These key questions represent areas that require exploration. It would be quite unwise to ask the questions as bluntly as written here.

What are your investment objectives?

What is your investment history/background?

What amount of money do you have to invest?

What is your current brokerage/bank relationship(s).

What is your primary financial need?

Investment Objectives

What are your investment objectives?

What would you like your money to do for you and your family?

Most people are interested in either growth, income, or tax-advantaged products. Which would you be most interested in?

Have you taken care of your future needs? How?

How have you addressed the problem of inflation?

Describe the ideal investment. What are its risk/reward characteristics?

Investment History

Have you ever been involved in the financial markets?

How about currently? Which areas? How have you done?

When was your investment program last reviewed?

What stocks do you own? Why did you purchase them?

What was the cost of your last purchase?

How have you done in the markets?

How do you hedge your risks?

Available Investment Dollars

The selection of an appropriate investment is partially dependent upon the amount of money available for investment. How much money are we talking about?

What is the current market value of your portfolio?

Where are your stocks located?

Would you be interested in generating additional cash flow?

What is the combined income of your family? Do you have adequate monetary reserves? How about your insurance coverage?

How much discretionary money is available?

How would you describe your approach to investments?

Brokerage Affiliation

Who is your current broker? How did you get together?

How long have you been dealing with that firm?

Have you dealt with any others in the past? Why did you change?

Are you completely satisfied with your current broker?

What are the things that you like the best?

How might your broker improve?

What can I do to earn your investment business?

If I gave you an idea that made sense, would you buy it from me?

Is your current broker fulfilling your needs?

Growth

Define growth.

Relate to risk.

What type of growth do you want? Need? Have you taken inflation into account? What is your expectation of inflation?

How much time are you going to allow to achieve your goals? What risk are you willing to take?

What would you consider to be a growth investment?

Income

Define income.

Parameters of income . . . Percentages acceptable.

Where is your money now?

What rate are you getting? What rates do you want?

Are you willing to sacrifice growth for income?

Do you want both growth and income?

What risks are you willing to assume?

What kind of assurances do you need?

What is your current and anticipated tax bracket?

Common Stock

What stocks do you own?

Number of shares? Price paid? Reason?

Have your stocks fulfilled their initial expectations?

What is the value of your portfolio?

Are your securities held in a single, joint, or margin account?

Do you have any loss carry-forwards?

What is your overall rate of return? Industry weightings?

When was your portfolio last reviewed?

Do you expect your portfolio to outperform the market? Why? Why not?

Bonds

What is your current and anticipated tax bracket?

What are your investment parameters—requirements for selection:
  Yield
  Yield to maturity
  Time till maturity
  Rating/protection features
  Items/areas/industries preferred
  Items/areas/industries that are unacceptable.

What is the purpose of your bond purchases?

Have you considered inflation?

Have you considered tax-bracket changes?

Have you considered risk?

Are you aware of yield-improvement techniques?

Are you aware of margin availability?

———

You should consider writing a dozen or so questions for each of the products and services with which your firm deals, since you will eventually have to fully qualify a prospect with respect to that product, service, or need. It is wise to prethink your questions. This allows you to more fully explore the client's needs and also makes you more professional.

You have been provided with a series of sample questions in a few areas on the previous pages. You might consider writing additional questions in areas such as:

Retirement planning

Educational funding

Investment needs

Estate planning

Retirement planning

Growth

Income

Tax-advantaged products

Risk

Inflation

Real estate

Income needs

Insurance needs

Taxes

Investment philosophy

Investment objectives

Stocks

Bonds

Mutual funds

Annuities

Margin

Option writing

Self-Critique Forms

It is frequently useful to review and critique your calls to determine your effectiveness. Periodically tape-record a prospecting or sales call and critique yourself on the forms below.

Cold Call Self-Evaluation

Identifying Data

Prospect Name: _____

Address: _____

Phone: _____

Business/Occupation: _____

Prospecting Track

Type of opener used? _____

Effective?   Yes _____   No _____

Overcame stalls or objections?   Yes _____   No _____

Qualified prospect?   Yes _____   No _____

Established a need I could fill?   Yes _____   No _____

What was the need? _____

Established rapport?   Yes _____   No _____

Closed for appointment or second call?   Yes _____   No _____

Date, time, and place of appointment/call? _____

_____

Literature to be mailed? _____

Asked for **referral?**   Yes _____   No _____

_____*Rapport Data*_____

Personality Type: Dictator   _____   Executive _____

                    Bureaucrat _____   Socialite   _____

Sensory mode: Visual   _____

                Auditory   _____

                Kinesthetic   _____

Buying criteria/motivations: _____

                             _____

                             _____

                             _____

                             _____

General Comments: _____

_____

_____

_____

Specific Plans for Improvement: _____

_____

_____

_____

Sales Call Self-Evaluation

Identifying Data

Client Name: _____

Address: _____

Phone: _____

Business/Occupation: _____

Sales Track
Opening

Benefit opener?	Yes _____	No _____

Benefit? _____

Reviewed parameters?	Yes _____	No _____
Matched features?	Yes _____	No _____

Presentation

Feature/benefit/probe?	Yes _____	No _____
Sizzle/story?	Yes _____	No _____
Repeated and justified key features?	Yes _____	No _____
Used caveats?	Yes _____	No _____
Made promises/guarantees?	Yes _____	No _____

Close

Benefit summary?	Yes _____	No _____
Probed for questions?	Yes _____	No _____
Answered all questions effectively?	Yes _____	No _____
Justified order size?	Yes _____	No _____
Asked for order?	Yes _____	No _____
Repeated order back to client?	Yes _____	No _____

Confirmation Call

Confirmed size, cost, and closing date of sale?	Yes _____	No _____

Asked for **referral?**   Yes _____   No _____

Psychological Profile

Used Psych Profile?   Yes _____   No _____

Type: Dictator _____   Executive _____

        Bureaucrat _____   Socialite _____

Used sensory mode?   Yes _____   No _____

Sensory mode: Visual   _____

               Auditory   _____

               Kinesthetic _____

Used buying criteria/motivations?   Yes _____   No _____

Buying criteria/motivations: _____

_____

_____

_____

_____

General Comments:_____

_____

_____

_____

Specific Plans for Improvement: _____

_____

_____

_____

Bibliography

Alessandra, Anthony J., Ph.D., and Phillip S. Wexler. *Non-Manipulative Selling*. Reston, Va.: Reston Publishing Company, 1978.

Bandler, Richard, and John Grinder. *Frogs into Princes*. Moat: Real People Press, 1979.

Bennett, Robert F. *Gaining Control: Your Key to Freedom and Success*. Salt Lake City: The Franklin Institute, 1987.

Bettger, Frank. *How I Raised Myself from Failure to Success in Selling*. New York: Cornerstone Library, 1949.

Blanchard, Kenneth, Ph.D., and Spencer Johnson, M.D. *The One Minute Manager*. New York: Berkley Books, 1982.

Buzzotta, V. R., Ph.D., R. E. Lefton, Ph.D., and Manuel Sherberg. *Effective Selling Through Psychology*. Cambridge, Mass.: Ballinger Publishing Company, 1982.

Carnegie, Dale. *How to Win Friends and Influence People*. New York: Simon and Schuster, 1981.

Dunn, Paul H. *Win if You Will*. Salt Lake City: Bookcraft, 1964.

Dunn, Paul H. *Meaningful Living*. Salt Lake City: Bookcraft, 1968.

Eliot, Robert S., M.D., and Dennis L. Breo. *Is It Worth Dying For?* New York: Bantam Books, 1984.

Frankl, Viktor. *Man's Search for Meaning*. New York: Washington Square Press, 1984.

Garfield, Charles. *Peak Performers: The New Heroes of American Business*. New York: William Morrow and Company, 1986.

Hampden-Turner, Charles. *Maps of the Mind: Charts and Concepts of the Mind and Its Labyrinths*. New York: Macmillan Publishing Company, 1981.

Hanson, Peter G., M.D. *The Joy of Stress*. New York: Andrews, McMeel and Parker, 1986.

Harris, Louis. *Inside America*. New York: Random House, 1987.

Harvard Business Review: On Human Relations. New York: Harper & Row, 1979.

Hill, Napoleon. *Think and Grow Rich*. New York: Fawcett Crest, 1960.

Hopkins, Tom. *How to Master the Art of Selling*. New York: Warner Books, 1982.

Kelly, Eugene A. *For What It's Worth: A Guide for New Stockbrokers*. Thomasville, Ga.: Marshwinds Advisory Company, 1984.

Laborde, Genie. *Influencing with Integrity*. Palo Alto, Cal.: Syntony Publishing, 1983.

Lynch, Dudley. *Your High-Performance Business Brain: An Operator's Manual*. Englewood Cliffs, N.J.: Prentice Hall, 1984.

Mackenzie, R. Alec. *The Time Trap*. New York: American Management Association, 1972.

Mager, Robert F. *Goal Analysis*. Belmont, Cal.: Fearon Publishers, 1965.

Maltz, Maxwell, M.D. *Psychocybernetics.* North Hollywood, Cal.: Wilshire Books Company, 1960.

Mandino, Og. *The Greatest Salesmen in the World.* New York: Bantam Books, 1985.

Molloy, John T. *New Dress for Success.* New York: Warner Books, 1988.

Naisbitt, John. *Megatrends.* New York: Warner Books, 1984.

Peale, Norman V. *The Power of Positive Thinking.* Englewood Cliffs, N.J.: Prentice Hall, 1952.

Peale, Norman V. *A Guide to Confident Living.* Englewood Cliffs, N.J.: Prentice Hall, 1948.

Peters, Thomas J., and Robert N. Waterman, Jr. *In Search of Excellence.* New York: Warner Books, 1981.

Raudsepp, Eugene, and Joseph Yaeger. *How to Sell New Ideas.* Englewood Cliffs, N.J.: Prentice Hall, 1981.

Robbins, Anthony. *Unlimited Power.* New York: Simon and Schuster, 1986.

Selye, Hans, M.D. *Stress Without Distress.* New York: Signet, 1974.

Selye, Hans, M.D. *The Stress of Life.* New York: McGraw-Hill Book Company, 1976.

Shafiroff, Martin D., and Robert L. Shook. *Successful Telephone Selling in the 80's.* New York: Barnes & Noble Books, 1982.

Shook, Robert. *Ten Greatest Salespersons—What They Say About Selling.* New York: Harper & Row, 1980.

Sill, Sterling W. *The Laws of Success.* Salt Lake City: Deseret Book Company, 1977.

Sill, Sterling W. *The Law of the Harvest.* Bountiful: Horizon Publishers, 1980.

Stanley, Thomas J. *Marketing to the Affluent.* Homewood, Ill.: Dow Jones-Irwin, 1988.

Winwood, Richard I. *Excellence Through Time Management.* Salt Lake City: The Franklin Institute, 1985.

Winter, Richard E., M.D., ed. *Coping With Executive Stress.* New York: McGraw-Hill Book Company, 1983.

Yaeger, Joseph, Ph.D. *Thinking About Thinking With NLP.* Cupertino, Cal.: Meta Publications, 1985.

Zigler, Zig. *See You at the Top.* Gretna: Pelican Publishing Company, 1977.

Index